EXPEDITIONS 3

A Course in Social Studies

Series Editor

Padmini Sriraman

Collins

3

EXPEDITIONS

A Course in Social Studies

Series Editor

Padmini Sriraman

Published by Collins India
A division of HarperCollins*Publishers* India Private Limited

HarperCollins *Publishers*
A-75, Sector 57, Noida,
Uttar Pradesh 201301, India
1 London Bridge Street, London, SE1 9GF, United Kingdom
2 Bloor Street East, Toronto, Ontario M4W 1A8, Canada
Lvl 13, 201 Elizabeth Street (PO Box A565, NSW, 1235), Sydney NSW 2000, Australia
195 Broadway, New York, NY 10007, USA

Browse the complete Collins catalogue at **www.collins.in**

First published in 2016
Latest reprint edition 2017

Reprinted: 10 9 8 7 6 5 4 3

ISBN: 978-93-5136-8-656

Content developed by **PreQuel**

Artwork and layout by **Quadrum Solutions**

Printed and bound in India by
Thomson Press India Ltd.

MRP: ₹ 224

Acknowledgements

Cover: Henu Studio Private Limited

Title Page: Henu Studio Private Limited

Inside: **Page 7**: ChrisGorgio; **8**: mapichai, Hollygraphic; **9**: 3DSculptor, solarseven, Vadim Svirin; **11**: ChrisGorgio; **12**: Hollygraphic, Hollygraphic, Hong Li; **13**: skegbydave, mapichai; **14**: AndrewJohnson; **18**: kapulya; **19**: molotovcoketail; **20**: slobo, snapphoto; **23**: malerapaso, janceluch, Photograpther, NickS, EduLeite, Gudella, thumb, GoodLifeStudio, wellglad, digpro, StockPhotosArt, Gannet77; **25**: Grafissimo; **26**: Marcus Lindstrom, Tomacco; **28**: chris_tack, cindygoff, panumas nikomkai; **29**: RakicN, daizuoxin; **30**: triloks; **31**: Simplyphotos, nikkytok, sundown001; **32**: artisticco, Achudo, luoman; **35**: Marcus Lindstrom; **39**: RNMitra, Utopia_88; **40**: erick4x4, Harjeet Singh Narang, master2; **41**: Korovin; **42**: ultramarinfoto; **46**: AravindTeki; **50**: Holger Mette; **51**: IndiaImages, Meinzahn, bpperry; **52**: shekhardino; **54**: narvikk; **56**: KishoreJ; **57**: botulinum21, saiko3p, naveen0301, Fabio Lavarone; **58**: naveen0301; **60**: LSP1982, Lou Jones Lonely Planet Images; **62**: neelsky; **63**: Danielrao, RNMitra, SoumenNath; **66**: DavorLovincic; **71**: mukesh-kumar; **72**: typhoonski, Focal.Point, rvrobinson; **73**: Kevin Clogstoun Lonely Planet Images; **74**: stockillustration; **75**: Amy_Lv; **76**: vbel71; **77**: Skouatroulio, Himanshu Lahkar; **78**: AravindTeki, elifranssens, yogesh_more; **80**: Lya_Cattel; **82**: tonyja44; **83**: PG-1973, Pgiam; **84**: davincidig; **85**: pagadesign, DNY59; **87**: 3DSculptor, awayge; **89**: highviews, Barcin, JamieRogers1; **90**: cnythzl; **92**: urfinguss, ImageDB; **94**: Brendan McIlhargey, mukesh-kumar, maayeka, DianePeacock, highviews, foryouinf; **96**: sbhaumik; **98**: JackQ, triloks; **101**: SHAUN CURRY, sadikgulec, Medini, Ashwin82, Matthew Wakem, pixitive, ajaykampani; **103**: CRSHELARE; **106**: Pattie Calfy, Bartosz Hadyniak, Max_Xie, Ekely, traveler1116, jstephenlee; **108**: okeyphotos; **109**: Hulton Archive, ilovethirdplanet; **110**: Ashwin, Tim Graham; **111**: ullstein bild; **113**: zanskar; **115**: rickszczechowski, dja65; **116**: sabirmallick, curtoicurto, subtik, Pshenichka, Sujay Govindaraj; **119**: isaxar; **121**: indianeye; **122**: lilly3, Floriana, Floriana; **125**: subtik; **127**: JelenaAloskina;
Maps © Collins Bartholomew Ltd 2016

Preface

If I cannot learn the way you teach, teach the way I can learn.

Expeditions is a comprehensive course in Environmental Studies and Social Studies for the primary school. This series for classes 1 to 5 has been designed taking into account the multidisciplinary nature of Environmental Studies. Following an interactive approach, the series caters for the young learners through inferential and experiential tasks, and stimulating content. The need for sustainable development holds the key to the future of mankind and young learners need to be sensitized to it through a gradual study to build environmental and social awareness. Therefore, in sync with the requirements of the curricula, books 1 and 2 offer a course in Environmental Studies and books 3 to 5 in Social Studies.

Expeditions is based on the underlying principle of the National Curriculum Framework that every learner can learn. This series maximizes opportunities to learn through its wide variety of tasks and facilitates easy learning and comprehension of the concepts at the primary level. Multiple intelligence-based tasks cater to the needs of all learners. With a learner-centric approach for effective teaching and learning in the classroom, the series promotes experiential learning. Course materials take off from the learner's prior knowledge and draw examples from real-life situations to foster knowledge building and understanding in them. The series provides ample scope for the learners to observe, reflect, hone their thinking skills and develop effective communication skills. Learners are guided to look at the environment in a holistic manner and see the underlying unity in the physical and social environment.

Key Features

- **I Know** assesses the prior knowledge of the learners.
- **Observe and Reflect** has pre-reading tasks that allow the learners to infer and relate to the topic.
- **Fact Zone** provides interesting titbits of information and **Find Out** tasks encourage referencing skills.
- **Do It Yourself** contains application-based activities for experiential learning.
- **Eco Zone** sensitizes learners towards conservation of environment.
- **Words Zone**, **Remember** and **Review Zone** at the end of the units facilitate understanding, recall and reinforcement, and assessment.
- **Think Zone** focuses on Higher Order Thinking Skills.
- **Life Skills Zone** equips learners with the basic skills they need to excel in life and **Value Zone** helps to build the right attitudes and values in learners.
- **Activity Zone** has varied creative tasks and **My Zone** helps in self-assessment and provides interesting **Pin It Up** activities.
- **Fun Time** has varied games and tasks for formative assessment.

The comprehensive teacher's resource materials are aimed at facilitating teaching and assessment. Feedback and suggestions to improve the course further are welcome.

Key Features

I Know ...

- Farmers use a .... to carry wheat to the flour mill.
- The fastest means of communication is the ....

Assesses the prior knowledge of the learners

Observe and Reflect

- What do you see in the picture?
- How do camels help people in deserts?
- Why is this animal called the ship of the desert?

Has warm-up tasks that initiates the learners into the topic and help them relate to it

Fact Zone

There are almost 1,54,866 post offices in India.

Provides interesting titbits of information

Find Out

When was the first aeroplane invented and by whom?

Tasks to encourage referencing skills

Eco Zone

Delhi is the most polluted city in the world. Efforts are being made to check the pollution.

Sensitizes learners towards conservation of environment

Value Zone

Use polite words like 'please' and 'thank you' while talking to community helpers.

Helps to build the right attitudes and values in learners

Remember

» The Earth can be called a unique planet because it is the only planet that has all the conditions necessary to support life.

» Lithosphere is made up of the outer crust, mantle and core.

Is a ready reckoner of the chapter

Life Skills Zone

Fill in the blanks with the correct answers.

1. Amit is working in Mumbai.
   He has to go to Delhi immediately.
   Which means of transport should he use?
   a. Car b. Ship c. Aeroplane

Equips learners with the basic skills they need to excel in life

Words Zone

magma: molten rock

alloy: a metal formed by mixing two types of metals together

dissolved: solid mixed with liquid and becoming a part of it

sleet: a mixture of rain and snow

Gives meanings of difficult words to facilitate understanding

Pin It Up

Make a list of the telephone numbers of the helpers who come to your home and pin it up on the board.

Useful fun tasks for learners

Activity Zone

FA

Make a photo frame

1. Take four lolly sticks and paint them. Paste them together as shown.
2. Decorate the frame with ribbons or shells.
3. Stick a ribbon on the backside

Has varied creative tasks

Review Zone

A **Fill in the blanks with the correct answers.**

1. If someone says that the day is hot and sunny then they are talking about the ....
   i. weather
   ii. climate
   iii. temperature
2. The climate of a place depends upon the ....
   i. month
   ii. season
   iii. type of landform

Reinforces the learning and facilitates assessment

Do It Yourself

FA

Take a glass. Pour a little squash in it. Then pour cold water and stir with a spoon. Listen to the sound of the spoon touching the glass while stirring. Smell the squash and taste the drink.

Name the organs that helped you to:

- see the things needed to make the drink ....
- feel whether the water is cold or not ....
- listen to the clink sound of the spoon in the glass ....

Activities for learners to attempt on their own

Think Zone

A What do you think would happen if the political divisions of India were dissolved? Discuss in class.

B **Look at the picture and answer the questions.**

1. What do you see in the picture?
2. What is this called?
3. Where can these be found in India?

Focuses on Higher Order Thinking Skills

SA — COMPREHENSIVE ASSESSMENTS

E Name the food items. (5)

F Answer the following questions. (10)

1. Why do we eat food?
2. Who lives in a small family?
3. When do we wear woollen clothes?
4. Why do we wear clothes?
5. What is a *pucca* house ?

G Match the pictures with the people. (5)

Assessments facilitate evaluation

My Zone

Draw a smiley if you know and a star if you wish to know more.

1. I know that many people help us in our daily life. ....
2. I know that we must respect and be polite to them. ....

Helps in self-assessment

FA — FUN TIME 1

Go on a space expedition! Roll the dice and play this game. If you don't know the answer, miss a turn. Watch out for bonus blocks!

Has varied games and tasks for formative assessment

Collins DigiSuite is an innovative digital solution for teachers. It contains four modules delivering classroom content that can be used to effectively integrate the teaching and evaluation tools with the coursebooks.

The **E-book** includes animations, interactive exercises and worksheets. The E-book reader also includes interactive teaching tools like pen tool, text highlighter, page zoom, search and bookmark.

The **Test Generator** is a question bank with a variety of questions for effective evaluation. It is an easy-to-use assessment tool for the teachers to create test papers and worksheets.

The **Teacher's Resource** consists of lesson plans, answer keys and teaching techniques for the teachers.

This module has a PDF of the **Collins Dictionary** appropriate for each level with all the words and definitions one needs.

Contents

1 The Universe

I Know ...

- We live on planet ...., which is a part of the ....
- The Earth has .... that we breathe and .... that we drink.

Observe and Reflect

- What gives light to all the other planets in our solar system?
- Identify it in the picture.
- What will happen if it is not there?

Have you ever observed the sky? The Sun shines brightly during the day. If you look at the night sky, you will find small, twinkling stars dotting the night sky and the moon glowing white. The Sun, moon and stars along with the planets are called **heavenly** or **celestial bodies**.

The Universe

The universe is a huge open space that holds everything. All living things, the Sun, planets, moons, stars, galaxies and dust clouds together make up the **universe**.

A **galaxy** contains planets, stars, dust and gases. There are many galaxies in our universe.

Fact Zone

Scientists believe that the universe was a hot bubble of dust and gases many, many years ago. A huge explosion known as the **Big Bang** occurred. As a result, all the gases and dust joined together to form the galaxies, stars, planets and other heavenly bodies in the universe.

Solar System

The Sun, its family of planets, their satellites or

moons, and other heavenly bodies like asteroids and comets form the **solar system**. The solar system is a part of the **Milky Way** galaxy. There are eight planets in the solar system. They are Mercury, Venus, Earth, Mars, Jupiter, Saturn, Uranus and Neptune.

The Sun is at the centre and the planets move around the Sun. The Earth is the third planet from the Sun. It is the only planet that has air and water—the conditions necessary to support life.

Planets

Planets move in a specific path called the **orbit** around the Sun. Each planet moves in its own orbit. This movement is called **revolution**. The Earth also spins like a top on its own **axis**. This movement is called **rotation**.

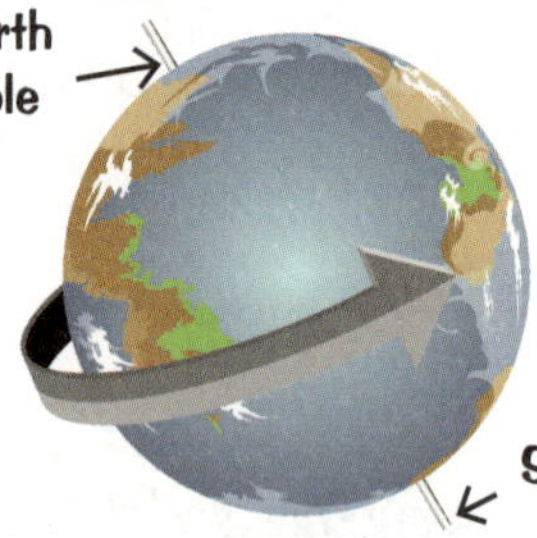

Planet Earth

We know our solar system has eight planets that move around the Sun. They get heat and light from the Sun. Mercury is the closest planet to the Sun and Neptune is the farthest planet. Jupiter is the largest planet of the solar system.

Stars

Stars are huge balls of hot gases. They have their own heat and light. They are huge in size but appear small because they are very far from us. The Sun is also a star. It is the closest star to the Earth, hence it appears so big. Stars, apart from the Sun, appear in the sky at night.

Difference between Planets and Stars

Planets	Stars
They have no light of their own.	They have their own light.
They move around the Sun.	They remain in a fixed place.
They are smaller than stars.	They are larger than planets.

Eco Zone

There is so much pollution on the Earth that the atmosphere which surrounds the Earth is thinning down letting in harmful rays of the Sun.

Interesting patterns formed by groups of stars are called **constellations**. Orion and Ursa Major are two well-known constellations.

Orion constellation

Satellites

Human-made satellite

Satellites are small, celestial objects that move around a planet. The moon is a natural satellite of the Earth. It moves around the Earth along a specific path or orbit. Some planets have more than one satellite. Jupiter has 67 satellites!

Satellites moving in space can be natural or man-made. Human-made satellites are sent into space to gather information about planets and for communication.

Comets and Asteroids

Comets are small celestial bodies that move around the Sun in a definite direction. They are made up of dust and ice.

Comet

Asteroids are rocky, celestial bodies that are too small to be called planets. They are often called minor planets. Most of the asteroids in the solar system are found between Mars and Jupiter.

Find Out

Who was the first Indian woman to go to space?

FA

Do It Yourself

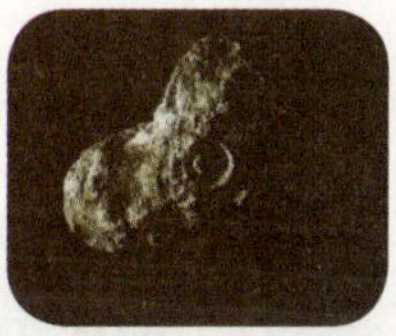

1. This object is a part of our solar system. Identify it.
2. Write any two things that you know about this object.

Remember

- The universe is a huge space where all the planets, galaxies, stars and other heavenly bodies are present.
- The Sun is at the centre of the solar system.
- There are eight planets in the solar system.

Words Zone

heavenly bodies: a planet, star or other natural objects that are visible in the sky

celestial: related to the sky

axis: an imaginary line running through the centre of a planet, around which it turns

- Stars have their own light and are bigger than planets.

Review Zone

A **Fill in the blanks with the correct answers.**

1. Our solar system is a part of the .... galaxy.
   a. Milky Way b. Orion c. Ursa Major
2. Interesting patterns formed by groups of stars are called ....
   a. galaxies b. constellations c. orbits
3. Planets move around the Sun in specific paths known as ....
   a. orbits b. streets c. satellites
4. Jupiter is the largest planet and it has .... moons.
   a. 67 b. 24 c. 80
5. Comets are made up of dust and ....
   a. water b. fire c. ice

B **Match the columns.**

Column A	Column B
1. Sun	a. Galaxy
2. Moon	b. Star
3. Milky Way	c. Fixed path
4. Orbit	d. Satellite

C **Answer these questions in brief.**

1. What do you understand by the term 'universe'?
2. What are heavenly bodies?
3. What is revolution?
4. What is rotation?
5. What is an axis?

D **Read the clues and complete the crossword with the names of the celestial bodies.**

Across

2. A small celestial body made up of dust and ice that moves around the Sun in a definite direction
3. Third planet from the Sun
4. A system of stars, dust and gases held together
5. Rocky celestial bodies that are too small to be called planets
7. Earth's satellite

Down

1. A group of stars that form a pattern
6. Closest star to the Earth

E **Answer these questions in detail.**

1. What are planets?
2. State the differences between planets and stars.
3. What are comets and asteroids?
4. What are satellites?

Think Zone

FA

A We know that the Sun is also a star. But why do we see the Sun only in the daytime and not at night along with the other stars?

B Identify this planet from our solar system. What sets it apart from other planets in the solar system?

Life Skills Zone

Would you leave Earth to live on any other planet? If yes, which planet would you choose? Give reasons for your answer.

Value Zone

The Earth is a unique planet. We must respect all its elements such as air, water and land.

Activity Zone

FA

Look at the constellations and name them using the words from the help box.

Help box
Taurus
Orion
Big Dipper

....

....

....

My Zone

FA

Draw a smiley if you know and a star if you wish to know more.

1. I know about the solar system. ....
2. I know the differences between stars and planets. ....
3. I know about natural and artificial satellites in space. ....
4. I know about asteroids and comets. ....

Pin It Up

Collect pictures of the first space travel and paste them on a drawing sheet. Name the country that launched the first spacecraft.

2 The Planet Earth

I Know ...

- The Earth belongs to the solar system along with .... other planets.
- The Earth is the .... planet from the Sun.

Observe and Reflect

FA

- What do you think the blue part is?
- What do you think the green areas are?
- What moves around the Earth?

In the olden days, people were afraid to travel or sail too far from their homes. They believed that the Earth was flat and if they travelled or sailed too far, they would fall off the edge of the Earth!

However, some people believed that the Earth was round. Ferdinand Magellan was the first person to prove this fact. In the early 1500s, he set out to sail around the world. He kept sailing westward and after three years the ship and its **crew** found itself back at the starting point. This proved that the Earth was round.

^ The Earth is round

However, the Earth is not a perfect circle, it appears to be flat at the top and the bottom. This shape is called an **oblate spheroid**. The flat part at the top is called the North Pole and the flat part at the bottom is called the South Pole.

Why There Is Life on the Earth

The Earth is often called unique since it is the only planet in the solar system that has the conditions necessary to support life. It has air, water and the right **temperature**.

Air

All living things need air to breathe. The Earth is surrounded by a layer of air called the atmosphere. The atmosphere surrounds the Earth like a thick blanket. It is made up of gases—oxygen, carbon dioxide and nitrogen—which are necessary for life.

Find Out

Recently, scientists have found signs that suggest that there is water on planet Mars. Find out more about this.

Water

The Earth is the only planet that has water. Like air, water is also essential for all living things to live. Water covers 70 per cent of the Earth's **surface** and the rest of the 30 per cent is covered by land.

Water percentage on the Earth

Temperature

The right temperature is required to survive on the Earth. The planet is located at such a distance from the Sun that the Earth's temperature is neither too hot nor too cold. During the day, clouds block part of the Sun's rays and at night, the clouds do not let the Earth's heat to escape.

The Blue Planet

From outer space, the Earth looks like a giant, blue ball with some green patches. It is called the 'blue planet' because of the abundance of water on its surface. The Earth is made up of land and water, that is, continents and oceans.

Continents

The Earth is divided into huge **land masses**. These land masses are called continents. There are seven continents on the Earth. Asia is the largest continent followed by Africa, North America, South America, Antarctica, Europe and Australia. Each continent has many countries.

Oceans

An ocean is a very large mass of water covering a huge part of the Earth's surface.

The oceans are the largest water bodies on the surface of the Earth. There are five oceans. They are the Arctic Ocean, the Atlantic Ocean, the Pacific Ocean, the Indian Ocean and the Southern Ocean. The Pacific Ocean is the largest ocean.

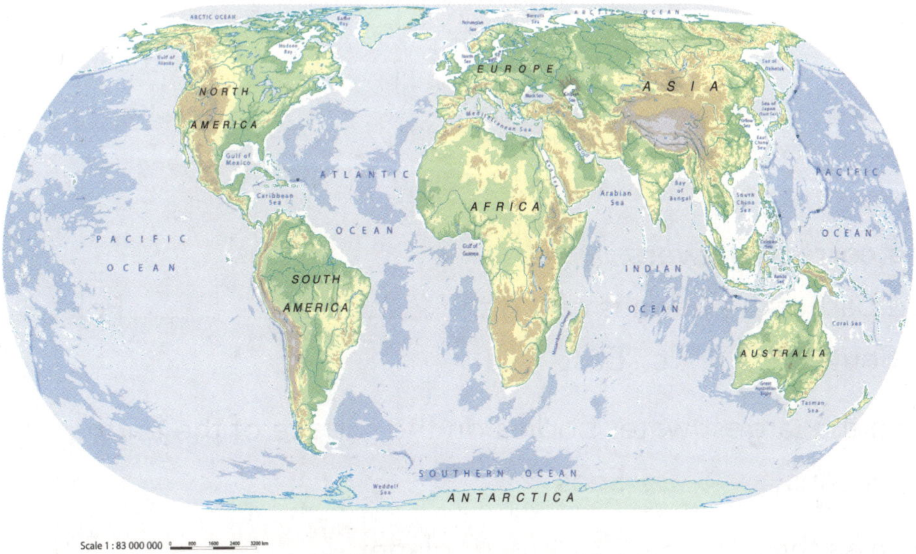

Continents and oceans of the world

Fact Zone

The Indian Ocean is the only ocean that is named after a country.

Eco Zone

Too much smoke in the air is making the Earth hotter every year.

FA

Do It Yourself

Complete the table with the name of one plant and animal found in these zones.

Place	Plant	Animal
Mountains		
Plains		
Deserts		

Remember

- The shape of the Earth is an oblate spheroid.
- The Earth has unique features like air, water and the right temperature that make life on the Earth possible.

Words Zone

crew: people who work on a ship

temperature: how hot or cold a place is

surface: the top layer of something

land mass: a large area of land

- The Earth is also known as the blue planet.
- There are five oceans and seven continents in the world.

Review Zone

A Fill in the blanks with the correct answers.

1. The northern flattened part of the Earth is called the .... Pole.
   a. North b. South c. East
2. .... are the largest water bodies on the surface of the Earth.
   a. Lakes b. Oceans c. Seas
3. The Earth is also known as the .... planet.
   a. red b. golden c. blue
4. Most of the Earth is covered with ....
   a. water b. land c. trees
5. There are .... continents on the Earth.
   a. five b. eight c. seven

B Write T for True and F for False.

1. The clouds block part of the sunlight during the day. ☐
2. There are six continents in the world. ☐
3. The Earth is not completely round. ☐
4. The temperature on the Earth is very hot. ☐
5. Water covers 30 per cent of the Earth's surface. ☐

C Unscramble the letters and write the continents on Earth in the word puzzle. Then, write the numbered letters in the order given and see which word you get.

1. SAAI ☐☐☐☐ (box 3 numbered 5)

2. RITSAALAU [8]

3. RACFAI [1]

4. PUOREE [7]

5. CANTAICART [3]

6. HORNT MAERACI [6 2]

7. UHSOT RIAACME [9 4]

1 2 3 4 5 6 7 3 8 9

D Answer these questions in brief.

1. What is the atmosphere?
2. What is the shape of the Earth called?
3. What is a continent?
4. Which is the largest ocean?

E Answer these questions in detail.

1. Name all the oceans of the world.
2. Name all the continents of the world.
3. Write a short note on the shape of the Earth.
4. How do clouds help in keeping the right temperature on the Earth?

Map Zone

On an outline map of the world, label the continents and oceans and colour it.

Think Zone

A How do you think the Earth's temperature would have been if clouds had not been there?

B **Look at the picture and answer the questions.**

1. Which landform do you see in the picture?
2. Name one such region in Asia and Europe each.

Life Skills Zone

The North Pole and South Pole are supposed to be extremely cold. How do you think animals and birds live there?

Value Zone

We must celebrate diversity and respect varied traditions, customs and beliefs of people in different regions of the world.

Activity Zone

Make an Earth Day Plaque

You will need blue and green coloured paper.

1. Cut a circle of the blue coloured paper.
2. Take the green coloured paper and trace the shape of the continents on it. Cut the green paper according to the outline you traced. Paste the green cutouts on to the blue circle. Does it look like the Earth?

My Zone

Draw a smiley if you know and a star if you wish to know more.

1. I know about the shape of the Earth. ....
2. I know why the Earth is unique. ....
3. I know about the continents and oceans on the Earth. ....

Pin It Up

Collect pictures of two unique things about each continent from old magazines and newspapers. Make a collage on a drawing sheet and label the images.

3 Finding Places

I Know ...

- We use a .... to find the direction of places.
- The Sun rises in the ....

Observe and Reflect

- Which direction has been marked in the picture?
- Mark the other three directions in the picture.

When you travel from home to school, do you go straight or do you turn left and right many times? People take different directions while travelling. North, east, south and west are known as **cardinal** directions. In addition, there are four more directions, namely, north-east, north-west, south-east and south-west. These lie between the four main directions and are called **sub-directions**.

Finding Directions

People use different ways to find places. During ancient times, people used the position of the Sun to determine directions.

An easy way to find directions when lost is with the help of a **compass**. A compass is used for the purpose of **navigation**. It has a needle that always points to the north. If we know one direction, it is easy to find the others.

Find Out

Who invented the compass? How is it different from the modern compass?

Do It Yourself

Look at the picture of the girl and answer the questions. She is facing the Sun and it is evening.

1. Which direction is on the right?
2. Which direction is on her left?
3. Which direction is she facing?

Sketch

Have you ever given someone directions to a place by drawing on a piece of paper? Such a drawing usually shows a small area with buildings and the road leading to a particular place. This is called a **sketch**. A sketch is a rough drawing that shows directions to a particular place.

Maps

Map

We use **maps** to find directions or places on the Earth. Maps are drawings of various parts of the Earth or the entire Earth on a flat surface. They cover a much larger area than a sketch. Maps show places that are very far from each other. This would be very difficult to fit in to a sheet of paper. For this reason, maps are drawn with a **scale** to represent the real distance between places. For example, a map might have a scale where 1 centimetre on the map is equal to 10,000 kilometres on the ground. Maps can be easily carried from one place to another.

Fact Zone

The world's largest atlas can be seen at the British Library in the United Kingdom.

A book of maps is called an **atlas**. An atlas has different types of maps.

Globe

A **globe** is a model of the Earth. The word 'globe' comes from the Latin word *globus*, which means a spherical object. We can see all the continents and oceans on a globe. However, we can only see one side of the Earth at a time. We will have to spin it around to see the other side. Globes are big and heavy to carry. That is why people use maps while travelling.

Globe

Difference between Maps and Globes

The differences between maps and globes are given in the table below.

Maps	Globes
Maps are drawn on a flat surface.	Globes are models of the Earth; they are round in shape and not flat.
A map does not show the shape of the Earth.	A globe shows the shape of the Earth.
A map is easier to use and can be taken anywhere.	A globe is heavy and difficult to carry to different places.
Maps show more **details** than globes.	Globes show fewer details than maps.

Remember

- There are four main directions—north, east, south and west.
- A compass is used to find directions.
- Maps can show almost any place on the Earth.
- An atlas is a book of maps.
- A globe is a model of the Earth.

Words Zone

cardinal: something that is important

navigation: the process of locating the place where one is at

detail: facts or features of something

Review Zone

A Fill in the blanks with the correct answers.

1. There are .... sub-directions.

   a. four   b. five   c. eight

2. A compass always points to the ....

   a. north   b. east   c. south

3. The word globe comes from the Latin word ....

   a. *globus*   b. *globule*   c. *global*

4. An atlas shows parts of the ....
   a. Earth   b. Mars   c. Sun

5. A compass is used for ....
   a. navigation   b. locating places on a map   c. locating places on a globe

B **Let us go on a treasure hunt. Follow the directions of the pirate map and trace the path with a red crayon to reach the treasure.**

1. From Start, move in the east direction past the Snake Pit.
2. Move south towards the Deep Hole and quickly go east, keeping the Skull Forest on your left.
3. Just before you reach the sea, head south towards the Dragon Mountains and Poison Lake.
4. Quickly move southwards between the Dragon Mountains and Poison Lake.
5. Make a quick dash to the west. As always, X marks the spot!

C **Answer these questions in brief.**

1. What is a sketch?
2. What is a globe?
3. What is an atlas?
4. Which is more detailed—a sketch or a map?
5. Name the cardinal directions.

D **Answer these questions in detail.**

1. How can one find directions with the help of a compass?
2. How are maps different from a sketch?
3. Why are globes not often used by travellers?
4. State two major differences between globes and maps.

Think Zone

A Which one do you think is more useful—maps or globes?

B **Look at the picture and answer the questions.**

1. What is this object known as?
2. What do the letters indicate?
3. How many cardinal and sub-directions can we see?

Life Skills Zone

Imagine you are going for an adventure. Look at the pictures and circle the things that you would take with you on the trip.

Value Zone

Always try to help people with directions if they are trying to locate a place.

Activity Zone

FA

Make a simple compass

You will need a bowl or a wide plastic cap, some water, a cork, a needle, a pair of scissors and a magnet.

1. Take the cork and ask an adult to slice a round piece using the scissors.
2. Take a sewing needle and rub it to a magnet twenty times in the same direction.

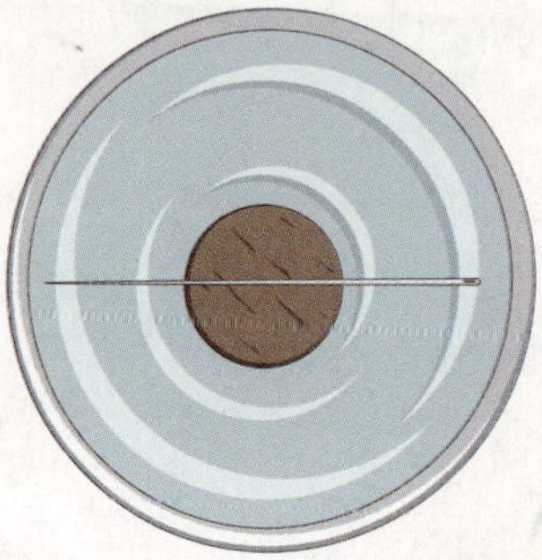

3. Take a bowl or a wide plastic cap. Add some water to it.
4. Place the round piece of cork in the center of the bowl of water.
5. Carefully place the needle on the cork and watch. The needle will slowly turn towards the north. Your compass is ready!

FA

My Zone

Draw a smiley 🙂 if you know and a star ⭐ if you wish to know more.

1. I know about all the directions. ....
2. I know about the different ways to find directions. ....
3. I know what sketches, maps and globes are. ....

Pin It Up

Find out the names of any two explorers who travelled by sea to far off places in the world. Write about the places they visited and paste their pictures on a drawing sheet.

4 Air on Earth

I Know ...

- Both plants and animals need .... to breathe.
- Air is present ....

Observe and Reflect

- What happens to a balloon when air is blown into it?
- Which would be heavier—an empty balloon or a balloon filled with air?
- Name two other things which we need to pump air into.

Air is all around us. We can feel it but we cannot see it. We need air to live. Plants and animals also need air to live.

Atmosphere

The Earth is surrounded by a layer of air called the **atmosphere**. The atmosphere is made up of different types of gases like oxygen, nitrogen and carbon dioxide. All of these gases are needed by living things to live.

Need for Atmosphere

All living beings need the atmosphere as it helps them in varied ways.

- The oxygen present in the atmosphere is necessary for humans, animals, birds and fish to breathe. We cannot live without oxygen.
- Plants need the carbon dioxide present in the atmosphere to make food. Animals and humans eat plants to stay alive.

- The Sun's light and heat make life possible on the Earth. It allows just enough heat to enter during the day and it does not let the heat escape at night. However, some of its rays can also harm us. The layer of atmosphere blocks out these harmful rays of the Sun and only lets in the necessary sunlight.

Fact Zone

The process of trapping heat by the Earth's atmosphere is called the greenhouse effect.

Air Pollution

Have you ever noticed that the air in the city smells different from that in the countryside? This is because air in most cities is **polluted**. Due to many human activities, harmful gases and substances are released in the air making it dirty. This is known as **air pollution**. We need clean and fresh air to breathe.

Eco Zone

Trees provide clean air to breathe. We must grow more trees.

Throwing garbage

There are many reasons why the air gets dirty and polluted. Smoke from factories, vehicles and burning of wood makes the air dirty. Throwing garbage out in the open and not **disposing** it properly also makes the air dirty. When we burn garbage, smoke is released, which adds to air pollution.

If we breathe in dirty air, we can fall sick. Air pollution can cause cough, **nausea**, irritation in the eyes and breathing problems. The air also becomes hotter, increasing the Earth's temperature.

Do It Yourself

Look at the picture and answer the questions.

1. What is being shown in the picture?
2. Can this be called a source of air pollution?
3. How do you think it can harm us?

Preventive Measures

There are several ways to prevent air pollution.

- We should plant trees in and around our homes because plants let out oxygen and make the air clean.
- We should avoid bursting crackers.
- We should walk more and avoid travelling by vehicles.
- We should dispose garbage in a proper place.
- We should always cover our mouth while sneezing or coughing.

Find Out

What is acid rain?

Remember

- The Earth is surrounded by a layer of air called atmosphere.
- All living things need air to live.
- Air pollution is caused when the Earth's atmosphere becomes dirty.
- Polluted air can make us sick.
- We should keep the air clean.

Words Zone

polluted: dirty and harmful substances added to the air, land and water

disposing: to throw away something

nausea: the feeling that you get when you need to vomit

Review Zone

A Fill in the blanks with the correct answers.

1. The Earth's atmosphere blocks harmful rays that come from the ....

   a. moon b. Sun c. stars

2. .... that comes out from factories, vehicles and the burning of wood can cause air pollution.

   a. Dust b. Water c. Smoke

3. .... air can make us sick.

   a. Polluted b. Clean c. Fresh

4. Plants need .... to make food.

   a. oxygen b. carbon dioxide c. nitrogen

5. We should always .... our mouth while coughing or sneezing.

a. wipe b. open c. cover

B **Match the columns.**

Column A	Column B
1. Atmosphere	a. Necessary for life
2. Oxygen	b. Smoke
3. Air pollution	c. Let out oxygen
4. Plants	d. Surrounds the Earth

C **Answer these questions in brief.**

1. What is air pollution?
2. What do plants need to make food?
3. What do factories let out?
4. What kind of air do we need to breathe?
5. What do plants let out?

D **Answer these questions in detail.**

1. What causes air pollution?
2. What is the Earth's atmosphere made up of?
3. How can we keep the air clean?

Think Zone

A It is said that factories cause pollution, but can we live without factories? What do you think should be done to control the air pollution caused by factories?

B Identify the causes of air pollution in the pictures and circle them.

Life Skills Zone

Find out the things that cause pollution at home. Make a list of these things and write what you should do to change it.

Value Zone

FA

Burning trash or leaves increases air pollution. Encourage gardeners and adults to create a compost pit for the disposal of waste.

Activity Zone

FA

Moving air

You will need a zip lock plastic bag, cello tape, a drinking straw and a small pom pom or ball.

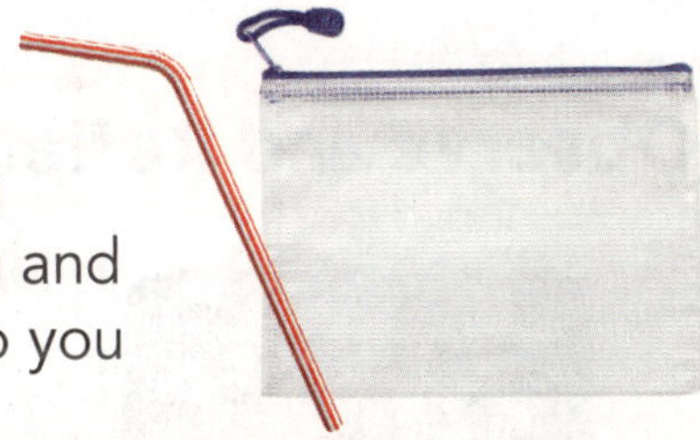

Take the zip lock plastic bag. Insert a drinking straw in the bag leaving one end of the straw outside the bag. Zip lock the bag and seal it with cello tape. Blow into the bag through the straw. Do you see the bag becoming big with air?

Place the pom pom or the ball on the table. Press the bag so that air from the straw blows towards the pom pom. Do you see it moving away from its position? Can you feel the air from the bag?

My Zone

Draw a smiley 🙂 if you know and a star ⭐ if you wish to know more.

1. I know about the atmosphere. ....
2. I know why all living beings need the atmosphere. ....
3. I know how air pollution can harm us. ....

Pin It Up

FA

Draw a picture showing the ways in which air gets polluted. On a sheet of paper, list the methods to keep the air clean.

5 Water on Earth

I Know ...

- .... per cent of the Earth is made up of water.
- We must .... water for the future.

Observe and Reflect

- What is happening in this picture?
- Is it right to waste anything?
- What would you do if you saw this?

We have learned how most of the Earth's surface is covered by water. In fact, there is more water on the Earth than land. Would it have been better if there was more land so we could build our homes on it? The answer is no. All living things need water to live. We need water just like we need food and air to **survive**.

Need for Water

Water is one of the most useful **resources** that we get from nature.

- Humans and animals drink water, while plants get water from the ground and air.
- Apart from drinking, water is used for cooking, bathing, washing clothes and dishes and many other activities.

Fact Zone

Seventy per cent of our body weight is made up of water.

- Water is important for growing crops.
- Electricity is also produced from water. It is known as hydroelectricity.

Forms of Water

Water is mainly available in three forms—**solid**, **liquid** and **gas**.

Water in a river

Steam coming out of a pot of boiling water

A frozen lake

The water that we get from seas, oceans, rivers and lakes is in the liquid form. When water becomes too hot, it **evaporates** to become water vapour, the gaseous form of water. When it cools down, it freezes and turns into ice. This is the solid form of water.

FA

Do It Yourself

Let us do an activity to see all forms of water.

Ask an adult to boil water in a kettle. Look at the vapour rising from the kettle once the water is boiled. This is the gaseous form of water.

Pour some water in an ice tray or a bowl and keep it in the freezer. Observe it after two hours. You will see water in the frozen form as ice.

Take the ice and put it on a plate. It will melt after some time and you will see water in the liquid form.

Water Cycle

The process through which water changes its various forms in nature is known as the **water cycle**.

- The process starts when the Sun's rays heat up the water in ponds, lakes, rivers, seas and oceans.
- The warm water evaporates to form water vapour.
- The water vapour rises up in the atmosphere. After reaching a great height, the water vapour changes into tiny drops of water.

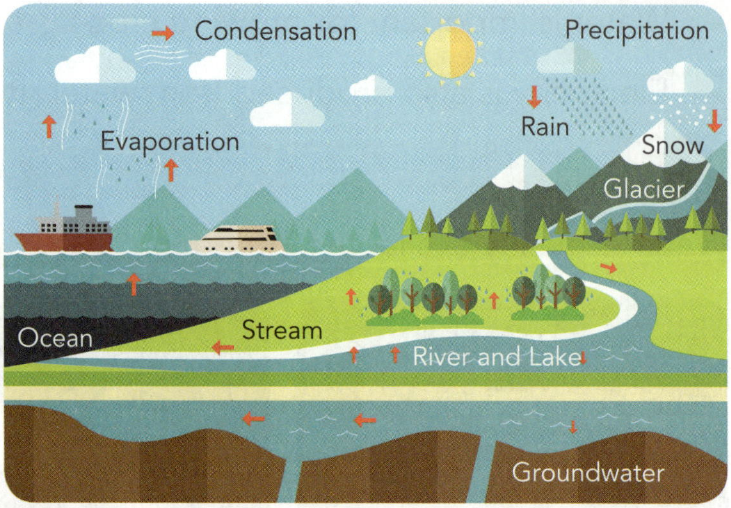

- Upon cooling, the tiny water droplets join to form clouds. This process is called **condensation**.
- When clouds become too heavy they burst and fall down on Earth as rain or snow. This is known as **precipitation**.

Find Out

Where do snowstorms occur in India?

Sources of Water

There are various sources of water.

Name four sources of water.

....

We know that water can be found underground as well. This is called **groundwater**. Man-made hand pumps, tube wells and wells are used to draw underground water. Dams and tanks are used to store water for later use.

Tube well

Water Pollution

The water that flows down as rivers from mountains is clean and pure, but as it enters the plains it becomes polluted. When various water bodies like rivers, lakes, oceans, seas and ponds get **contaminated** by the collection of harmful chemicals in them, it is known as **water pollution**.

Polluted water

Many factors cause water pollution. Washing clothes and utensils, bathing animals and throwing waste on the banks of rivers and ponds are major causes of water pollution. Harmful substances released from factories pollute streams and rivers. The seas and oceans get polluted due to oil spills or leakage from ships.

We can prevent water pollution by not disposing waste and plastic bags in rivers, ponds and other sources of water. Factories should not be allowed to release harmful chemical wastes into water bodies.

Eco Zone

Fish and other creatures cannot survive once the river becomes polluted.

Clean Drinking Water

Water from oceans and seas is not used for drinking as it is too salty. Freshwater from rivers, lakes and water stored underground is used for drinking. But one cannot drink this water directly from the source. It has to be **purified** before being used for drinking. People use filters to purify water.

Fact Zone

Only 2.5 per cent of the water on Earth can be used for drinking.

Save Water

Water is very precious, hence it should not be wasted. We should save water. Rainfall is one of the most important sources of water both in villages and cities. During the rainy season, most of the rainwater runs off the roads and terraces into drains. We can store this rainwater and use it later. This is known as **rainwater harvesting**.

Remember

- Water is available in three forms—solid, liquid and gas.
- The process through which water changes its various forms in nature is known as the water cycle.
- Water pollution occurs when water bodies get contaminated.
- We should drink clean water and not waste it.

Words Zone

survive: to continue to live

resource: something that a country can use, which increases their wealth

evaporate: when water turns into water vapour

contaminated: polluted

purified: made pure and clean

Review Zone

A Fill in the blanks with the correct answers.

1. The most basic use of water is ....
   a. drinking b. bathing c. washing
2. Water turns into .... when it freezes.
   a. water vapour b. ice c. sand
3. Water gets heated up due to the rays of the ....
   a. moon b. star c. Sun
4. .... are used for drawing underground water.
   a. Wells b. Dams c. Lakes

B Circle ten sources of water in the wordsearch.

Glacier
Handpump
Lake
Pond
Rain
River
Sea
Snow
Spring
Well

U	H	I	M	S	N	O	W	L	O	F	B	E	E	I
Z	R	Y	P	X	B	O	Q	A	M	Q	H	N	A	R
H	A	N	D	P	U	M	P	K	E	T	N	T	U	S
Q	Y	X	V	K	O	O	Q	E	U	A	N	T	Q	B
U	A	S	S	Y	A	J	C	I	M	N	F	O	H	W
F	S	P	N	E	D	P	T	I	R	B	W	Z	T	A
Q	A	R	Y	V	A	F	O	E	F	K	H	J	J	K
Z	K	I	F	K	W	M	V	N	C	S	G	U	E	O
U	H	N	O	D	C	I	G	I	D	V	H	D	Y	V
Y	J	G	A	T	R	G	Q	L	X	F	S	U	G	A
Q	B	G	T	X	H	P	T	W	A	U	L	P	M	U
A	J	Y	F	N	S	R	E	K	N	C	J	A	J	M
B	F	D	I	Q	P	X	J	A	Q	O	I	G	Y	Y
P	V	A	U	K	T	Z	W	E	L	L	N	E	R	P
N	R	A	A	C	T	J	C	R	T	I	M	I	R	V

C **Answer these questions in brief.**

1. What is water pollution?
2. What is the gaseous form of water called?
3. Name the different sources of water.
4. State two causes of water pollution.

D **Answer these questions in detail.**

1. Why do we need water?
2. How can we prevent water pollution?
3. Describe the water cycle with a diagram.

Think Zone

FA

A The water in seas and oceans is too salty and unfit for drinking. Why can't we drink salt water?

B **Look at the picture and answer the questions.**

1. What is being shown in the picture?
2. If someone drank this water, what would happen?
3. What steps can be taken to clean this water body?

Life Skills Zone

How do you think throwing waste into lakes and rivers would affect the water creatures living there?

Value Zone

Keep some water in a clay dish in your balcony or outside for the birds. You can do the same in parks for stray cats and dogs.

Activity Zone

FA

Prepare a chart mentioning the various ways in which water gets polluted. Paste pictures along with each point.

My Zone

Draw a smiley if you know and a star if you wish to know more.

1. I know why we need water. ....
2. I know about the different sources and forms of water. ....
3. I know we must keep water clean and should save water. ....
4. I know we should save water as it is a precious resource. ....

Pin It Up

Collect pictures of things that pollute water. Paste them on a sheet of paper and pin it up. Remember not to throw these things in the water.

Assessment 1 (Chapters 1-5)

Maximum Marks: 25

A Fill in the blanks. (1 × 8 = 8)

1. The Earth revolves around the ....
2. .... was the first to prove that the Earth is round.
3. East is a .... direction.
4. The .... is like a blanket surrounding the Earth.
5. Water found underground is called ....
6. .... is when tiny droplets of water join to form clouds.
7. Smoke from factories, vehicles and burning of wood makes the air ....
8. We should avoid bursting ....

B Match the columns. (1 × 10 = 10)

Column A	Column B
1. Used for communication	a. Navigation
2. Largest ocean in the world	b. Filter
3. Rainfall	c. Sub-direction
4. A gas used by plants to make food	d. Comet
5. North-west	e. Star
6. Made up of ice	f. Satellite
7. Made of hot gases	g. Collection of maps
8. Compass	h. Precipitation
9. Purified water	i. Pacific
10. Atlas	j. Carbon dioxide

C Tick (✓) the appropriate answer. (1 × 7 = 7)

1. Which of these do we get from rivers and lakes?
   a. Salt water   b. Freshwater
2. Which type of air is good for us?
   a. Clean   b. Polluted
3. Which of these provides more details about a place?
   a. Globe   b. Map
4. Which of these are named after a country?
   a. Atlantic Ocean   b. Indian Ocean
5. What are found between Mars and Jupiter?
   a. Comets   b. Asteroids
6. Which of these is caused by pollution?
   a Nausea   b. Stomach ache
7. Which of these should we do?
   a. Save water   b. Waste water

6 India: Physical

I Know ...

- We live in the beautiful country named ....
- Our country has the Himalayan mountains in the .... (south/north).

Observe and Reflect

Look at the map of India. It shows the natural landforms in different colours. Name the colours used to represent these in the map.

- Mountains ....
- Plains ....
- Desert ....
- Plateau ....

When we look at the map of India, we find that our country has different types of landforms—the snow-covered Himalayas, the hot sandy Thar Desert, the Ganga Plains, the long sandy beaches of Goa, the thick Sundarban forests and the beautiful islands of Lakshadweep. This is why India is called a land of great **diversity**.

Fact Zone

The southern part of India is surrounded by an ocean on three sides. This type of landform is known as a **peninsula**.

Look at the map given on the next page. You will find India has six natural or physical regions:

- The Northern Mountains
- The Northern Plains
- The Deccan Plateau
- The Thar Desert
- The Coastal Plains
- The Island Regions

The Northern Mountains

The Great Himalayan Range, the world's highest mountain range, runs along the northern part of India. Mount Everest, the world's highest mountain peak, is located in this range.

The Himalayas are an important physical feature of India. The snow from these mountains melts giving rise to rivers like Ganga, Yamuna, Indus and Brahmaputra.

Kanchenjunga

This mountain range protects India from the cold winds blowing from the north. The Himalayan forests are a source of medicinal herbs and timber. Many hill stations such as Mussoorie, Nainital, Shimla and Darjeeling are located in the lower slopes of the Himalayas.

The Northern Plains

The **Northern Plains** lie to the south of the Himalayas. They are vast **fertile** plains suitable for **cultivation** and are thickly populated. The main rivers of this region are Ganga, Indus and Brahmaputra.

> **Find Out**
>
> Name any two famous mountain peaks of the Himalayas.

Northern Plains

The Northern Plains are very fertile and provide food for the entire country. This region is also called the **bread basket of India**. The rivers flowing through the plains provide water for **irrigation** throughout the year. Plains are also suitable for building cities and towns. The capital of India, New Delhi, is located in the Northern Plains.

The Deccan Plateau

Deccan Plateau

A **plateau** is an area of flat land that is higher than the land around it. It is also called a **tableland** as it resembles a table. The Deccan Plateau is located in the southern part of India. The plateau region is important as its fast flowing rivers are used to generate electricity. The southern plateau is also a **storehouse of minerals** as a variety of mineral deposits are found here. The Deccan region is covered with fertile black soil, which is suitable for the growth of cotton.

The Thar Desert

The Thar Desert

The north-western part of India is covered by a vast sandy desert known as the **Thar Desert** or the **Great Indian Desert**. The whole of Rajasthan and some parts of Gujarat make up the desert region. This region receives very less rainfall and very few trees grow here. Due to such conditions, deserts have very few people living there.

The Coastal Plains

Land that lies along a coast is called a **coastal plain**. Narrow strips of coastal plains are found on both sides of the southern part of India. These are called the **Eastern Coastal Plain** and the **Western Coastal Plain**.

Eco Zone

Each natural region of India is known for its unique fauna and flora.

Lakshadweep Islands

The Island Regions

An island is a piece of land that is surrounded by water on all sides. India has two large island groups—Andaman and Nicobar Islands and the Lakshadweep Islands. The Andaman and Nicobar Islands lie in the east in the Bay of Bengal. The Lakshadweep Islands lie in the west in the Arabian Sea.

FA

Do It Yourself

A coral reef is a community of living things made up of different types of plants and fish living deep in the ocean. The Lakshadweep Islands are home to some of the largest coral reefs in the Indian Ocean. What kind of plants are found there?

Remember

- India has many natural landforms.
- India can be divided into six physical regions: the Northern Mountains, the Northern Plains, the Deccan Plateau, the Thar Desert, the Coastal Plains and the Island Regions.

Words Zone

diversity: the state of having a wide range of differences

fertile: land or soil where plants grow well

cultivation: growing crops

irrigation: the process of supplying water to an area for the purpose of planting crops

Review Zone

A. Fill in the blanks with the correct answers.

1. The highest mountain peak in the world is Mount ....
   a. Himalayas b. Everest c. Shiwalik
2. Another name for plateau is ....
   a. coast b. Deccan c. tableland
3. The Eastern Coastal Plains lie in the ....
   a. east b. west c. south
4. The Thar Desert lies in the ....
   a. east b. west c. north

B **Write T for True and F for False.**

1. Mussoorie is located along the Eastern Coastal Plains. ☐
2. Island groups of India receive very little or no rainfall throughout the year. ☐
3. The Thar Desert covers parts of Rajasthan and the whole of Gujarat. ☐
4. India has many diverse landforms. ☐
5. The Himalayas protect India from cold winds coming from the south. ☐

C **Answer these questions in brief.**

1. Why do people prefer to live in the Northern Plains?
2. Why are the Himalayas important to us?
3. What is meant by a peninsula?
4. Name the main east and west flowing rivers of the plateau region.

D **Answer these questions in detail.**

1. Why is the desert region of India thinly populated?
2. Why are the Northern Plains known as the bread basket of India?

Map Zone

Label the natural divisions of India on an outline map of India.

Think Zone

FA

Look at the picture below. The Himalayas are a major attraction for people interested in adventure sports like white river rafting, paragliding and skiing.

1. Find out the different types of adventure sports that people do in the mountain regions.
2. Do you think these sports activities are safe? Would you ever take up such activities? Discuss your answer in class.

Life Skills Zone

India has some of the most beautiful beaches in the world. Find out about some famous beaches of India. What should you do to protect the beaches?

Value Zone

Rivers are the lifeline of the regions to which they belong. We must keep them clean.

Activity Zone

FA

Fill in the columns with one thing from each of these places.

Place	Plant	Animal	Bird	Food
Northern Mountains				
Northern Plains				
Thar Desert				
Deccan Plateau				
Coastal Plains				
Islands				

My Zone

FA

Draw a smiley if you know and a star if you wish to know more.

1. I know about all the physical features of India. ....
2. I know about the Northern Mountains and plains in India. ....
3. I know about the plateau, desert, coastal plains and island regions of India. ....

Pin It Up

Collect pictures of five animals found in the sandy Thar Desert of India. Paste them on a sheet of paper and write their names.

7 India: Political

I Know ...

- I live in the state of .... in India.
- The capital city of my state is ....

Observe and Reflect

- Name the continent in which India lies.
- Name two countries situated near India.
- Name two water bodies that surround India.

If you look at the world map you will find that India is located in the southern part of the continent of Asia. Can you see the different countries surrounding India in the north, south, east and west? These are our neighbouring countries. India is surrounded by:

- Pakistan and Afghanistan in the north-west
- China and Nepal in the north and Bhutan in the north-east
- Bangladesh and Myanmar in the east
- Maldives and Sri Lanka in the south

India and its neighbours cover such a large portion of the globe that these countries taken together are known as a **subcontinent**.

Fact Zone

India is the seventh largest country of the world and is the second most populous country in the world.

Can you guess the name of the subcontinent? It is named after the largest country in the region. Yes, it is called the **Indian subcontinent**.

Political Divisions of India

India is a vast country with a large population. India has been divided into smaller regions known as **states**. There are 29 states in India and seven **union territories**. Each state has its own capital city and state government. Different states have their own special food, dress, language, festivals and dances.

The 29 states of India are Andhra Pradesh, Manipur, Arunachal Pradesh, Meghalaya, Assam, Mizoram, Bihar, Nagaland, Chhattisgarh, Odisha, Goa, Punjab, Gujarat, Rajasthan, Haryana, Sikkim, Himachal Pradesh, Tamil Nadu, Jammu and Kashmir, Telangana, Jharkhand, Tripura, Karnataka, Uttar Pradesh, Kerala, Uttarakhand, Madhya Pradesh, West Bengal and Maharashtra.

The seven union territories of India are the Andaman and Nicobar Islands, Chandigarh, Dadra and Nagar Haveli, Daman and Diu, the Lakshadweep Islands and Puducherry. The national capital region of Delhi is a special union territory of India.

Find Out

Which areas come under the NCR of Delhi?

Government in India

The **government** of India has two main levels—the central government and the state governments. Each state has its own government, while union territories are governed directly by the central government.

The Parliament House

All the important government houses are located in New Delhi, since it is the capital of India. The President and Prime Minister are the most important people in the national government. India is governed by the rules made in the Parliament which is located in New Delhi. In a state government, the Chief Minister and Governor are the most important people. In a union territory the Lieutenant-General is responsible for **governance**.

Find Out

Jharkhand, Uttarakhand and Chhattisgarh were formed in the year 2000. Name the newest formed state which was formed in 2014.

Local Government in Cities and Villages

The local government bodies take care of the smaller areas. The big cities of India are governed by the municipal corporations. Municipal corporations are local governing bodies that work for the development of a city. They collect tax and get money from the government and provide services like healthcare, transport, housing, educational institutions and many more. In smaller cities or towns, municipalities look after the facilities of the people. The states are divided into districts. These are further divided into blocks and villages. At the local level, the gram panchayat looks after the welfare of the people in the village.

Eco Zone

Chandigarh is one of the most cleanest cities in India.

Do It Yourself

Complete this quiz.

1. Which body makes laws for the country? ....
2. Which body provides healthcare? ....
3. Which body looks after the welfare of the people in villages? ....
4. Which body governs the state? ....

Remember

- India is located in Asia. It is the seventh largest country in the world.
- India is divided into 29 states and seven union territories.
- The government of India has two main levels—the central government and the state governments.
- In cities, municipal corporations look after the needs of the people.
- In villages, panchayats are responsible for managing matters.

Words Zone

government: the group of people that is responsible for managing the matters of a country or a state

governance: the process of managing the matters of a country/state/city/village

Review Zone

A Fill in the blanks with the correct answers.

1. .... lies to the north-west of India.
   a. Pakistan b. Nepal c. Bangladesh
2. There are .... union territories in India.
   a. five b. six c. seven
3. The Government of India is also known as the .... government.
   a. unified b. unitary c. union
4. The big cities are governed by ....
   a. municipal divisions b. municipal unions c. municipal corporations
5. The gram panchayat looks after the welfare of the people in the ....
   a. blocks b. districts c. villages

B Write T for True and F for False.

1. The union government looks after the union territories. ☐
2. In villages, the municipal corporations look after the people. ☐

3. Myanmar is located towards the north of India. ☐
4. Puducherry is a union territory. ☐
5. The union territories are governed by chief ministers and governors. ☐

C Answer these questions in brief.

1. How many countries border India?
2. How many states are there in India?
3. How many union territories are there in India?
4. Name the local government in cities.

D Answer these questions in detail.

1. Which countries make up the Indian subcontinent? Why has it been named so?
2. Write a short note on the system of governance in India.

Think Zone

FA

A Do you think that it is necessary to have different levels of government for governance? Give reasons for your answer.

B Look at the picture of the gram panchayat. List any two issues that may be discussed here.

Life Skills Zone

Find out more about the state where you live and tick (✓) accordingly.

1. Roads are good. ☐
2. There is no problem of power cuts. ☐
3. Heavy rains lead to floods. ☐
4. Earthquakes occur twice a year. ☐

Value Zone

We should respect laws and rules of our state. They are made to help us.

FA

Activity Zone

Unscramble the letters to get the names of 13 states of India. Take the letters that appear in the circled boxes.
Unscramble them to arrive at the name of the newest state of India.

1. MAHHRASARTA
2. LERKAA
3. RAUGAJT
4. NAAGALND
5. NABJUP
6. SASMA
7. RAAHYNA
8. TARHUANDTKA
9. LAGMAEHAY
10. MIZARMO
11. MIRUPNA

Answer

FA

My Zone

Draw a smiley if you know and a star if you wish to know more.

1. I know about all the states of India. ....
2. I know India has seven union territories. ....
3. I know the types of governments that govern at different levels in the country. ....

Pin It Up

Talk to three of your classmates who come from other states. Find out about their festivals, food, clothing, dance, language, etc. Make a table and fill in all the information on a sheet of paper.

8 North India: Delhi

I Know ...

- Delhi is a .... like Daman and Diu.
- .... is the capital of India.
- The president and prime minister of India live in ....

Observe and Reflect

- Name the monument.
- What happens here every year?
- The flag of which country gets hoisted every year at this place?

Every country has many big and small cities. One big city located on the banks of the Yamuna river is Delhi. Can you guess why it is important? Delhi is important because it is the capital of India.

The city is located in the northern part of India. To its west lies Haryana and to its east lies Uttar Pradesh. It is divided into two parts—Old Delhi and New Delhi. Most of Old Delhi lies along the Yamuna river. Delhi has grown over the years and is now called the **National Capital Region**.

Climate

Delhi has a very **extreme** climate. The summer season in Delhi lasts from April to October. These are very hot and dry months in which a hot and dry wind called **loo** blows. Monsoon arrives during the months of July and August. From November till February, Delhi experiences cold winters.

Historical Importance of Delhi

Delhi is a very important city. Since ancient days, the city has always been the seat of the Indian government. Both the Mughals and the British built beautiful **monuments** in the city.

Since New Delhi is the capital of India, all the important buildings of India, such as the Parliament House, Rashtrapati Bhavan (the place where the President of India lives) and the Supreme Court (the highest court of India) are located here.

Find Out

Although Delhi is one of the greenest cities in the world, yet, it is also one of the most polluted cities in the world. Why?

Major Tourist Attractions of Delhi

Delhi has a rich heritage of monuments and has often been described as a tourist's haven.

Tourist places of Delhi

Qutub Minar is one of the oldest monuments of Delhi. Located in south Delhi, it is India's second tallest minar. It is built in red stone and has five storeys. Within the same complex stands an iron pillar that has not **rusted** till date, even after hundreds of years.

The **Jama Masjid** is the largest mosque in India. It was built by the Mughal ruler, Shah Jahan. It is situated in Old Delhi and is made of white and red stone.

Jama Masjid

The **Red Fort** was built by the Mughal ruler, Shah Jahan, in red sandstone. Every year the Prime Minister hoists the Indian flag at the fort on Independence Day.

Old Delhi is also famous for its marketplace, **Chandni Chowk**. It is known for its *havelis*, wholesale markets, jewellery shops and street food.

The magnificent city of New Delhi built during the British rule is known for its **colonial** style buildings. **India Gate**, which is located at the centre of the city, is a memorial for soldiers who died in the First World War. The **Rashtrapati Bhavan**, the residence of the president of India, is located near India Gate at Rajpath. It is famous for its Mughal Gardens.

India Gate

Rashtrapati Bhavan

Fact Zone

The city of New Delhi also known as Lutyens' Delhi.

Eco Zone

Old Delhi has one of the oldest bird charity hospitals in Chandni Chowk, near the Red Fort.

Living in Delhi

Delhi has been called 'Little India'. People from all parts of India come to settle in the capital. Thus, Delhi is home to a diverse group of people with different traditions, cultures, religions and languages. Delhi is also a green city with wide roads lined with trees. It has many parks, gardens, shopping centres and stadiums. It has many well-known places of worship, such as the Akshardham Temple complex and the Lotus Temple. The city has one of the best airports in the world.

The modern day **Delhi Metro** is well connected. Every day hundreds of people travel across the city.

FA

Do It Yourself

Look at the picture and answer the questions.

1. What do you see in the picture?
2. Is it moving over ground or underground?
3. Is it faster than a car?

Remember

- Delhi is located in northern India on the banks of the Yamuna river.
- New Delhi is the national capital of India.
- Delhi experiences very hot and dry summers and very cold winters.
- Major tourist attractions in Delhi are the India Gate, Qutab Minar and Red Fort.

Words Zone

extreme: very great in degree; too hot or too cold

monument: a large structure built to remind people of someone or something famous

rust: reddish-brown substance that forms on some metals

» People from all parts of the country live in Delhi.

colonial: connected with or belonging to a country that controls another country

Review Zone

A Fill in the blanks with the correct answers.

1. Haryana lies to the .... of Delhi.
   a. west b. east c. north

2. .... built the Jama Masjid in Delhi.
   a. Akbar b. Jahangir c. Shah Jahan

3. The .... of India lives in Rashtrapati Bhavan.
   a. president b. chief minister c. prime minister

4. The prime minister hoists the national flag every year on Independence Day at the ....
   a. Rashtrapati Bhavan b. Red Fort c. Parliament

5. Qutub Minar is a .... -storeyed structure.
   a. five b. four c. six

B Match the columns.

Column A	Column B
1. Jama Masjid	a. Shah Jahan
2. Rashtrapati Bhavan	b. Largest mosque in India
3. Chandni Chowk	c. Memorial for soldiers
4. India Gate	d. Residence of the president of India
5. Red Fort	e. *Havelis*

C Write T for True and F for False.

1. During Mughal rule, Delhi was the capital. ☐

2. Red Fort was built by the British.

3. New Delhi is the capital of the National Capital Territory of Delhi.

4. Rashtrapati Bhavan is located in Rajpath.

D Answer these questions in brief.

1. Who built the Jama Masjid?
2. What kind of climate does Delhi have?
3. Delhi is located on the banks of which river?
4. What is the capital of the National Capital Territory of Delhi?

E Answer these questions in detail.

1. Why is Delhi considered an important city?
2. Why is Delhi called 'Little India'?
3. Describe any two tourist attractions of Delhi.

Map Zone

On an outline map of Delhi, locate two important places of Delhi.

Think Zone

FA

A Delhi is a tourist's haven. There are many old buildings in Delhi like the Qutub Minar, Red Fort, Jama Masjid and so on. What do you think needs to be done to protect these buildings from being damaged?

B Look at the picture and answer the questions.

1. What are the two monuments shown in the picture?
2. State an interesting fact about any one of the monuments shown in the picture.

Life Skills Zone

Imagine your cousin has come to visit you for the first time. She wants to visit the green places of Delhi. Name any two places where you would take her to.

Value Zone

FA

Monuments were built by workers over a period of many years. Appreciate their work and take a pledge to keep the monuments clean.

Activity Zone

FA

Work in groups and try to visit a monument. Write a report on the monument mentioning its name, the type, colour, how is it maintained, signboards in the monument and any special feature of the place.

My Zone

FA

Draw a smiley if you know and a star if you wish to know more.

1. I know that Delhi is the capital city of India and is a very important city. ....
2. I know that there are many historical buildings in Delhi. ....
3. I know that we should keep the city clean. ....

Pin It Up

Which is your favourite place in Delhi? Collect pictures of the place and paste it on a sheet of paper. Write two sentences about why you like this place.

9 West India: Mumbai

I Know ...

- Mumbai is a city located in the state of ....
- The old name of Mumbai is ....
- The Bollywood industry is located in ....

Observe and Reflect

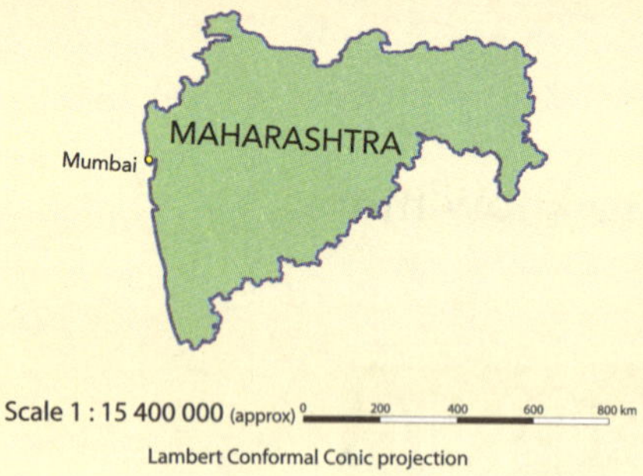

- What is the capital of this state?
- In which part of India is this state located?
- What is it famous for?

Mumbai is a very famous city of India. It is the capital of the state of Maharashtra and it is made up of seven islands.

Climate

The climate of Mumbai is wet and dry. The summer season begins in March and ends in June. From July onwards, the rainy season starts and continues till September. October and November are relatively dry months. The winter season lasts from December to February. Since Mumbai is near the Arabian Sea, the weather remains **humid** and it never becomes too hot or too cold.

Gateway of India

Historical Importance of Mumbai

The city was called Bombay by the British, who ruled over India for more than 200 years. In 1995, its name was changed to Mumbai after the Goddess Mumba Devi.

Mumbai is one of the most important **ports** in the country. It is home to many industries like textiles, chemicals, oil and medicines. The first passenger railway line in India was laid in Mumbai. Now, Mumbai is regarded as the **financial**, entertainment and **commercial** capital of India.

Bombay High

Mumbai is also important because of the oil deposits off the coast of Mumbai. This region is known as Bombay High.

Major Tourist Attractions of Mumbai

Tourist places of Mumbai

Some places have become major landmarks of Mumbai. Located at a natural **harbour**, the Gateway of India is the most famous landmark of Mumbai. It was built by the British to welcome Queen Mary and King George V to India. It has four towers with stone carvings on them.

Nearby are the Elephanta Caves located on the island of Elephanta, almost 10 km away from the city. One has to take a **ferry** from the Gateway of India to reach the Elephanta Caves. The caves are huge temple structures carved out from rocks, believed to be built in memory of Lord Shiva.

Elephanta Caves

Marine Drive is a beautiful stretch of road running along the coast of Mumbai. Known as the queen's necklace, the road sparkles at night when the street lights lining the coast are lit up.

Queen's necklace

The recently built Sea Link or the Bandra-Worli Sea Link is a 5.6 km long bridge.

Bandra-Worli Sea Link

Eco Zone

Noise pollution is one of the major issues that Mumbai is facing.

Living in Mumbai

Since it is a **metropolitan** city, people from all corners of India live in Mumbai. The local people of Mumbai are called Maharashtrians. Marathi, Gujarati, Konkani, Hindi and English are the commonly spoken languages.

Find Out

Name two famous dishes of Mumbai.

Fact Zone

The Asiatic Society of Bombay is one of the oldest public libraries in the city.

Ganesh Chaturthi is the most important festival here. The city of Mumbai is known for its street food such as *pav bhaji* and *vada pav*. Mumbai has a strong network of local trains for people to travel across the city. The city is also known for the Wankhede Stadium.

Do It Yourself

1. What do you see in this picture?
2. What are the possible causes for it?
3. How does this affect the environment?

Remember

- Mumbai is the capital of Maharashtra.
- Mumbai is made of a group of seven islands.
- The Gateway of India, Marine Drive, Elephanta Caves and Sea Link are the major tourist attractions of Mumbai.
- Local trains are a common mode of transport for the people of Mumbai.

Words Zone

humid: warm and damp

port: a place where ships load and unload goods

financial: connected with money

commercial: connected with the buying and selling of things

harbour: a place on the coast where ships are kept

ferry: a boat or a ship that carries people

metropolitan: connected to a large city

Review Zone

A Fill in the blanks with the correct answers.

1. Maharashtra is located in .... India.
   a. western b. eastern c. southern

2. Mumbai is made of a group of .... islands.
   a. nine b. eight c. seven

3. The .... caves are located in Mumbai.
   a. Elephant b. Elephant's c. Elephanta

4. The other name of the Sea Link is .... Sea Link.
   a. Bandra-Worli b. Worli-Andheri c. Bandra-Thane

B Write T for True and F for False.

1. Trains are not available in Mumbai. ☐
2. Ganesh Chaturthi is an important festival in Mumbai. ☐
3. Mumbai has a dry climate. ☐
4. Mumbai is an important port. ☐
5. The Sea Link is also known as the queen's necklace. ☐

C Match the columns.

Column A	Column B
1. Ganesh Chaturthi	a. Lord Shiva
2. Oil	b. Street food
3. Marine Drive	c. Bombay High
4. *Pav bhaji*	d. An important festival
5. Elephanta Caves	e. Queen's necklace

D **Answer these questions in brief.**

1. Who built the Gateway of India?
2. Which goddess was Mumbai named after?
3. The Elephanta Caves are dedicated to which god?
4. What are the local people of Mumbai called?

E **Answer these questions in detail.**

1. Which is the common mode of transport in Mumbai?
2. Write a short note on the climate of Mumbai.
3. Describe the history of Mumbai.

Think Zone

FA

A Which is one of the most recurring natural disasters this city faces due to heavy rains?

B **Look at the picture and answer the questions.**

1. What is shown in the picture?
2. How is it different from a normal bus?
3. Which can hold more people—this one or a normal bus?

Life Skills Zone

Have you heard of the *dabbawala*, a person who delivers lunch boxes to working people in Mumbai? Find out how this unique system solves the problem of food for thousands of people in Mumbai.

Value Zone

FA

Many people living in slums in the city of Mumbai do not get proper education. Donate your old books to help these children study.

Activity Zone

FA

Prepare a travel booklet about the major tourist attractions of Mumbai other than the ones mentioned in the chapter. Paste pictures and add one or two lines about them. Your booklet should have at least four tourist attractions.

My Zone

FA

Draw a smiley if you know and a star if you wish to know more.

1. I know that Mumbai is the financial capital of India. ....
2. I know the important landmarks of the city of Mumbai. ....
3. I know about the people who live in Mumbai. ....

Pin It Up

Take a drawing sheet. Make a collage of the film studios in Mumbai with pictures from magazines.

10 East India: Kolkata

I Know ...

- .... is the capital of West Bengal.
- West Bengal lies in the .... part of India.

Observe and Reflect

- What do you see in the picture?
- On what does this vehicle run?
- Can this vehicle move anywhere on the road or does it move along a fixed path?

Kolkata is the capital of West Bengal, a state in eastern India. This important city is located on the banks of the Hooghly river. During British rule, Kolkata was the capital of India until it was shifted to Delhi.

Climate

Kolkata has a wet and dry climate. The summer season lasts from March to June and it is normally hot and humid. The rainy season lasts from July to September and at times it rains till October. The winter season starts in late November and goes on till February.

Historical Importance of Kolkata

Kolkata is the main centre of education, culture and **commerce** in eastern India. Though Kolkata is not located beside the sea, it lies on the

Fact Zone

The Calcutta High Court solves cases from Andaman and Nicobar Islands, apart from those of West Bengal.

banks of the river Hooghly, which meets the sea. Therefore, Kolkata is the oldest river port. Kolkata is also an important producer of jute products in India.

Major Tourist Attractions of Kolkata

Howrah Bridge

The Howrah Bridge is the pride of Kolkata. It is an **architectural** wonder built by the British. Also known as the Rabindra Setu, it covers the entire Hooghly river and connects Kolkata to Howrah. It is supported only by two pillars at the two ends and does not have pillars in the middle. This makes the bridge look as if it is hanging.

Find Out

Apart from the Howrah Bridge, there is another important bridge in Kolkata. Find out its name and when it was built.

The Victoria Memorial is perhaps the most famous landmark of Kolkata. This beautiful monument was built in white marble to honour Queen Victoria. It also has a museum.

Victoria Memorial

Fort William is a well-guarded fort built in 1781 by the British. It is still as beautiful as before and the Indian Army now uses it. Other places of interest in Kolkata are the Botanical Gardens where an ancient banyan tree can be found and the Alipore Zoo that is famous for its winter **migratory** birds.

Living in Kolkata

A majority of the people in Kolkata are Bengali. Bengali is the main language. However, Hindi and English are spoken as well. People use local buses, metro and taxis to travel in the city.

Tourist places of Kolkata

Bengali sweets such as *rosogolla* and *sandesh* are famous throughout the country. The most important festival of Kolkata is Durga Puja, which generally lasts for five days.

Durga Puja celebrations

Football is a very popular sport in Kolkata. The **Eden Gardens** and the **Salt Lake** are two of the most important stadiums of the city.

Eco Zone

The river Ganga is one of the most polluted rivers in India.

Remember

- Kolkata is the capital of West Bengal.
- The main tourist attractions of Kolkata are Howrah Bridge, Victoria Memorial, Fort William, Botanical Gardens and Alipore Zoo.
- The most important festival of Kolkata is Durga Puja.

Words Zone

commerce: the buying and selling of goods

architectural: related to architecture

migratory: people, animals or birds who move together in large groups from one place to another

Review Zone

A Fill in the blanks with the correct answers.

1. The rainy season in Kolkata starts in ....
   a. July b. August c. September
2. The Victoria Memorial was built using ....
   a. sandstone b. diamonds c. white marble
3. .... is the most important festival of Kolkata.
   a. Durga Puja b. Eid c. Christmas
4. A lot of migratory birds come to the ....
   a. Alipore Zoo b. Botanical Gardens c. Howrah Bridge

B Write T for True and F for False.

1. Kolkata is the capital of West Bengal. ☐
2. Kolkata has an extreme climate. ☐

3. Kolkata used to be the capital of British India. ☐

4. Botanical Gardens is famous for migratory birds. ☐

5. Local trains are not available in Kolkata. ☐

C Match the columns.

Column A	Column B
1. Durga Puja	a. Fort
2. Victoria Memorial	b. Festival
3. Rabindra Setu	c. Stadium
4. Fort William	d. Bridge
5. Eden Gardens	e. Monument

D Answer these questions in brief.

1. Which is the most important festival in Kolkata?
2. Where in India is Kolkata located?
3. What does the Howrah Bridge connect Kolkata to?
4. What modes of transport do people use to travel in Kolkata?

E Answer these questions in detail.

1. Discuss the location and climate of Kolkata.
2. Why is Kolkata regarded as an important city?
3. Which are the various landmarks of Kolkata?

Map Zone

Mark the Hooghly river on an outline map of Kolkata.

Think Zone

A Why do you think Kolkata still has modes of transport like trams that one may not find elsewhere?

B **Look at the picture and answer the questions.**

1. Identify the station shown in the picture.
2. In which city is it located?
3. Name another important station of this city.

Life Skills Zone

There are several modes of transport in Kolkata. Which amongst these would you choose and why?

Value Zone

Form an 'Eco club' and plant a sapling in your neighbourhood every week.

Activity Zone

Answer this Who Am I? quiz on Kolkata.

1. I am the garden where the ancient banyan tree is found. ....
2. I am the lightest, softest white sweet ball found in Kolkata. ....
3. Most people of Kolkata speak this language. ....
4. I have migratory birds as guests during winters. ....

My Zone

Draw a smiley if you know and a star if you wish to know more.

1. I know that Kolkata is the capital of West Bengal and that it is a river port of eastern India. ....
2. I know that there are many historical buildings in the city of Kolkata. ....
3. I know about the people of Kolkata. ....

Pin It Up

Collect pictures of some of the famous bridges of India and paste them on a chart paper.

Assessment 2 (Chapters 6-10)

Maximum Marks: 25

A Fill in the blanks. (1 x 8 = 8)

1. The prime minister of India lives in the city of ....
2. Eden Gardens is located in the city of ....
3. .... is a favourite sport of Kolkata.
4. The Sea Link is .... long.
5. The .... is the largest mosque of India.
6. The first passenger railway line in India was laid in ....
7. The Akshardham Temple is located in ....
8. .... is a war memorial for soldiers who died in the First World War.

B Match the columns. (1 x 10 = 10)

Column A	Column B
1. A flat land higher than all land around it	a. Delhi
2. An Indian state formed in 2000	b. Northern Plains
3. A city to have metro railway	c. Ganesh Chaturthi
4. A city by Yamuna river	d. Kolkata
5. Film stars	e. Fort
6. Newest state of India	f. Plateau
7. Most important festival of Mumbai	g. Bollywood
8. Fort William	h. *Rosogolla*
9. Bread basket of India	i. Telangana
10. A Bengali sweet	j. Jharkhand

C Tick (✓) the appropriate answer. (1 x 7 = 7)

1. Which of these islands can be found in the Arabian Sea?
   a. Andaman and Nicobar b. Lakshadweep
2. Where does the president of India live?
   a. Delhi b. Mumbai
3. Who governs the union territories?
   a. King of India b. Central government of India
4. The Elephanta Caves were built in whose memory?
   a. Lord Buddha b. Lord Shiva
5. Gram panchayats look after whom?
   a. City dwellers b. Villagers
6. Who is responsible for the government of union territories?
   a. Chief Minister b. Lieutenant-General
7. Which of these is the highest mountain peak in the world?
   a. Mt Everest b. Himalayas

Go on a space expedition! Roll the dice and play this game. If you don't know the answer, miss a turn. Watch out for bonus blocks!

Comprehensive Assessment 1 (Chapters 1-10)

Maximum Marks: 50

A Put a tick (✓) near the correct option. **(1 x 10 = 10)**

1. Which of the following is a sub-direction?
   a. south-west b. south
2. Which of the following is a continent?
   a. Pacific b. Europe
3. Which of these are at the centre of the solar system?
   a. Earth b. Sun
4. Which of these are used by navigators to find directions?
   a. telescope b. compass
5. What are groups of stars that make a pattern in the sky called?
   a. constellation b. galaxy
6. Which type of water do we drink?
   a. salty water b. freshwater
7. Which of these is part of air?
   a. sulphur b. oxygen
8. Which of these is necessary for plants to make food?
   a. oxygen b. carbon dioxide
9. Which of these is surrounded by water from all sides?
   a. tableland b. island
10. Which of these is our neighbour in the east?
    a. Bangladesh b. China

B Match the columns. **(1 x 5 = 5)**

Column A	Column B
1. A symptom of pollution	a. Water
2. Moves around the planets	b. Nainital
3. 70% of the Earth is covered by this	c. Delhi
4. Lower slopes of Himalayas	d. Satellite
5. National capital of India	e. Nausea

C Find an odd one in each line and write the reason why it is odd. **(2 x 10 = 20)**

1. Earth — Jupiter — Venus — Moon
   Reason: ....
2. Oxygen — Nitrogen — *Rosogolla* — Carbon dioxide
   Reason: ....
3. Punjab — Uttar Pradesh — West Bengal — Puducherry
   Reason: ....
4. Chennai — Kolkata — Jharkhand — Mumbai
   Reason: ....
5. Nainital — Mumbai — Dehradun — Darjeeling
   Reason: ....
6. Gateway of India — Qutub Minar — Red Fort — Jama Masjid
   Reason: ....
7. Marathi — Konkani — Gujarati — English
   Reason: ....
8. *Rosogolla* — *Sandesh* — Hindi — *Biryani*
   Reason: ....
9. Sun — Earth — Moon — Mumbai
   Reason: ....
10. Asia — Europe — Atlantic — Antarctica
    Reason: ....

D Answer the following questions. **(3 x 5 = 15)**

1. We have learned how air and water are polluted. Write down five things you can do at home to prevent air and water pollution.
2. Write down all the information you can get about India by looking at a globe and compare it with the information you may get from a political map of India.
3. Why do you think people visit Nainital or Darjeeling in the summer season? Where are they located?
4. How are the Northern Plains and Coastal Plains different from each other?
5. Distinguish between a sketch and a map.

11 South India: Chennai

I Know ...

- Chennai is located in the .... part of India.
- Chennai was previously known as ....

Observe and Reflect

- What do you see in the picture?
- Name the food items that you know.
- Which ones do you like?

We have learned about the important cities in the north, west and east of India. In south India, Chennai is one of the most important cities. It is the capital of Tamil Nadu. It lies on the south-eastern coast of India, near the Bay of Bengal. It is located on the Coromandel Coast.

Climate

Chennai has a humid and warm climate almost throughout the year. The months of May and June are the hottest. January and December are the coolest months. It gets most of the rainfall between October and December.

Historical Importance of Chennai

Chennai is an old city. It has been ruled by many famous rulers including the Cholas. It was later visited by the Portuguese, the Dutch, the French and the

English traders. The British built their first building in India—**Fort St George**—in Chennai.

> ### Fact Zone
> Chennai is also known as the Gateway to south India.

Chennai is one of the most important educational, cultural and economic centres of south India. Like Mumbai, Chennai too has a large film industry. Many factories and industries are based in Chennai. It also has a successful **automobile** industry which is why it has been called the 'Detroit of India'.

Major Tourist Attractions of Chennai

Marina Beach

The city of Chennai is divided into two parts, the old city and the new city. The old city is also known as George Town. Anna Salai is the main road of Chennai.

There are several tourist attractions in Chennai. The **Marina Beach** is the second longest beach in the world and the end point of this beach is known as Elliot's beach. On the Marina Beach lies **St Thomas Church**. The biggest attraction of this church is the statue of Virgin Mary, which is believed to have been brought from Portugal a long time ago.

Kapaleeswarar Temple

Built by the British when they first came to India, **Fort St George** has a museum in one part. **Kapaleeswarar Temple** with its carved *gopuram* is one of the most famous and oldest temples in the city. The office of the Chennai Corporation, **Ripon building**, is an example of fine architecture.

Tourist places of Chennai

Guindy National Park is situated inside the city. It has a **Snake Park**, which is home to snakes of all kinds.

National Art Gallery in the Government Museum

There are several museums in Chennai, like the **Government Museum** and the **Birla Planetarium**. The Government Museum has a huge reading room and a total of 46 galleries.

> ### Eco Zone
> The Marina Beach was once famous for its rich ecosystems. Today, most parts of the beach have been deemed unusable due to pollution.

Living in Chennai

Most of the people in Chennai are Tamilians. Like other metros of India —Delhi, Mumbai and Kolkata—there are many people living here who do not belong to the state. There are people from Andhra Pradesh, Odisha, Goa, Karnataka, West Bengal, Punjab and Kerala, and **communities** such as Marwaris, Parsis, Sindhis and Anglo-Indians in Chennai. The people are fond of dance and music. A branch of Indian classical music known as Carnatic music originated in the city.

Tamil is the main language, but English is also spoken. Chennai is well connected by trains and city buses. Chennai is known for its south Indian food like *dosa*, *idli*, *vada*, *sambhar*, *appam*, *rasam*, which are now popular not only in India but also abroad. People are fond of rice and coconut in Chennai. Pongal is the most famous festival of Chennai.

Do It Yourself

Find out why the Vivekanada House and Museum is one of the most important museums in Chennai.

Remember

- Chennai is located in southern India and is the capital of Tamil Nadu.
- The British built their first building in India—Fort St George—in Chennai.
- The main tourist attractions of Chennai are Marina Beach, Ripon building, Snake Park, Government Museum and Kapaleeswarar Temple.

Words Zone

automobile: cars and vehicles

communities: groups of people who share a common language or religion

Review Zone

A **Write T for True and F for False.**

1. All the four seasons are experienced in Chennai. ☐

2. Chennai is known as the Manchester of India.

3. Snake Park has a large variety of snakes.

4. Carnatic music originated in this city.

5. English is not spoken in Chennai.

B **Match the columns.**

Column A	Column B
1. Snake Park	a. Automobiles
2. Detroit of India	b. *Gopuram*
3. St Thomas Church	c. Guindy National Park
4. Kapaleeswarar Temple	d. Marina Beach

C **Answer these questions in brief.**

1. What kind of climate does Chennai have?
2. What did the British build in Chennai?
3. Why is Chennai called the 'Detroit of India'?
4. What are the various modes of transport available in Chennai?

D **Answer these questions in detail.**

1. Describe the food of the people of Chennai.
2. Describe the history of Chennai.
3. Write a short note on the major landmarks of Chennai.

Think Zone

FA

A Why do you think the British built Fort St George along the coast of Chennai?

B **Look at the picture and answer the questions.**

1. What do you see in this picture?
2. What is the design on the floor called?
3. Which festival is being celebrated?

Life Skills Zone

What kind of clothes do you think the people in Chennai wear according to the city's climate?

Value Zone

We should not litter along the shoreline in Marina Beach.

Activity Zone

FA

Make a coconut shell bowl

You will need one half of a coconut shell and sand paper.

1. Clean the coconut shell and rub it with the sand paper.
2. Sanding the coconut shell would take a lot of time so be prepared to work! When the rough outer layer of the coconut is smooth, wash the coconut shell. You now have a coconut shell bowl.

My Zone

FA

Draw a smiley if you know and a star if you wish to know more.

1. I know that Chennai is located in southern India and is the capital of Tamil Nadu. ....
2. I know that the main tourist attractions of Chennai are Marina Beach, Fort St George, Snake Park, St Thomas Church and Kapaleeswarar Temple. ....
3. I know that Chennai is famous for its south Indian food. ....

Pin It Up

Chennai is famous for its temples. Find their names, collect pictures and paste them on a sheet of paper.

12 More Indian Cities

I Know ...

- Bengaluru was earlier known as ....
- .... is the capital of two states of India—Punjab and Haryana.

Observe and Reflect

- What do you see in the picture?
- Are these people from India?
- Do they look happy celebrating together?

We have already learned about Delhi, Mumbai, Kolkata and Chennai. Now we will learn about the other cities of India.

Vidhana Soudha

Bengaluru is the capital of Karnataka. It is located in the southern part of India. The people in Bengaluru largely speak Kannada and English. Bengaluru has a pleasant climate throughout the year.

Many industries like aircraft, computers, electronic goods, machines, **textiles** and watches have **flourished** in this city. Bengaluru is also known as the Silicon Valley of India because it has many **IT** companies. The Vidhana Soudha, the seat of the state legislature of Karnataka is located in the city.

Fact Zone

Bengaluru is also called the Garden City.

The Government Museum, Tipu Sultan's palace, Lal Bagh, Vidhana Soudha, Chick Pet and Kempe Gowda Circle are some of the important tourist attractions of Bengaluru.

Find Out

What makes Cubbon Park one of the most important locations of Bengaluru?

If you look at the map of India you will find that **Chandigarh** is located in northern India. It is a union territory and serves as the capital of both Punjab and Haryana. The city was named after *Chandi*, a Hindu goddess.

Chandigarh was the first planned city of India after independence and hence, it is also known as the 'City Beautiful'. The Rock Garden of Chandigarh is famous for statues made out of waste materials. It also has the largest rose garden in Asia.

Rock Garden, Chandigarh

Guwahati is located in Assam in eastern India. It is one of the largest cities of eastern India and the biggest in Assam. The city is also known as the 'Gateway to North-east India'. It lies along the banks of the river Brahmaputra.

Assamese, English and Bangla are the major languages spoken here and Bihu is the most popular festival celebrated in the city. The woollen shawls and **handicrafts** of Guwahati are very well known. The state welcomes hundreds of people every year who visit to see the Kamakhya Temple, the Forest Museum and the State Museum.

Bihu dance

Hyderabad, which falls in the state of Telangana in southern India, is the shared capital of Andhra Pradesh and Telangana. People in this city speak English and Telugu. The Mecca Masjid, one of the largest mosques in the world, is located here. The Charminar, the most famous tourist attraction of Hyderabad, is located near the Mecca Masjid. People also visit the Birla Mandir, Ravindra Bharati and Salarjung Museum when they visit Hyderabad. The city is a major hub of the information technology industry.

Fact Zone

Hyderabad is also called the City of Pearls.

Do It Yourself

1. Name this famous building located in Hyderabad.
2. Find out in which part of the city does it lie—old or new.
3. What is the significance of the name of the building?

Jaipur is the capital of Rajasthan, which is situated in north-western India. Jaipur is known as the Pink City because a large number of houses are coloured pink in this city.

Hindi and English are the commonly spoken languages of the city. Jaipur is famous for its handicrafts like jewellery, tie-dye, metal and ivory work, and marbles.

Jaipur

Lucknow is the capital of Uttar Pradesh, located by the banks of the river Gomti.

Urdu, Hindi and English are the major languages spoken in the city. The **embroidery** work of Lucknow, also known as *chikankari*, is well known. Lucknow has many popular tourist destinations like Rumi Darwaza, the Imambaras, the Clock Tower and the Residency.

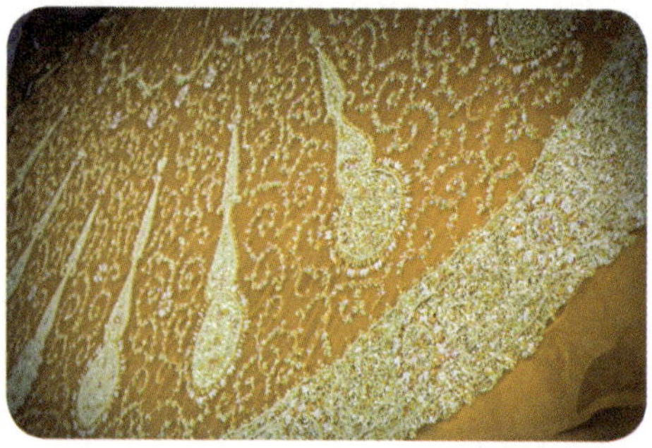

Chikankari work

Ahmedabad, also known as Amdavad locally, is located in Gujarat on the banks of the river Sabarmati. Ahmedabad is one of the quickest growing cities in India. It is known as the 'Manchester of the East' because of its growing textile industry. The Siddhi Bahir Mosque, the Kite Museum and the Sabarmati Ashram are some of the places of tourist interest.

Garba is a famous folk dance of this city, which people perform while celebrating Navratri. Famous dishes of the city are *dhokla* and *thepla*. Gujarati, English and Hindi are the languages spoken in the city.

Eco Zone

Heavy construction work is one of the major causes of pollution in Ahmedabad. The lack of green cover creates difficulty in controlling the the pollution levels there.

Remember

- Bengaluru is located in Karnataka.
- Chandigarh is the capital of both Punjab and Haryana.
- Guwahati in Assam is regarded as the Gateway to North-east India.
- Hyderabad is the capital of both Andhra Pradesh and Telangana.
- Jaipur is the capital of Rajasthan.
- Lucknow is well known for its embroidery work.
- Ahmedabad is well known for its textile industry.

Words Zone

textile: any type of cloth made by weaving or knitting

flourished: to become successful quickly

IT: information technology

handicrafts: making beautiful things using hands

embroidery: patterns that are sewn onto cloth using threads of various colours

Review Zone

A Fill in the blanks with the correct answers.

1. Bengaluru is the capital of ....
   a. Tamil Nadu b. Kerala c. Karnataka
2. Chandigarh is named after goddess ....
   a. *Durga* b. *Chandi* c. *Kali*
3. Guwahati is located by the river ....
   a. Ganga b. Yamuna c. Bramhaputra
4. The Charminar is located in ....
   a. Bangalore b. Hyderabad c. Lucknow

B Answer these questions in brief.

1. What is the capital of Karnataka?
2. Which city is famous for its *chikankari* work?
3. Where is the largest rose garden in Asia?

4. Why is Jaipur called the Pink City?
5. Which city is famous for its silk sarees?

C **Match the columns.**

	Column A		Column B
1.	Bengaluru	a.	City of Pearls
2.	Hyderabad	b.	Pink City
3.	Jaipur	c.	City Beautiful
4.	Chandigarh	d.	Gateway to North-east India
5.	Guwahati	e.	Garden City

D **Answer these questions in detail.**

1. Write a short note on Guwahati.
2. Write a few lines about Hyderabad.
3. Describe Jaipur in your own words.
4. Write a short note on Lucknow.
5. What do you know about Karnataka?

Map Zone

Label the cities you have studied about on a political map of India.

Think Zone

FA

A Of all the cities that you read about, which city would you say is the oldest? Give reasons for your answer.

B **Look at the picture and answer the questions.**

1. Identify the garden named after a flower.
2. In which Indian city is it located?
3. It is also the biggest in which part of the world?

Life Skills Zone

You know Chandigarh is the planned city of India. People face many problems while living in an unplanned city. Find out three difficulties that people face in such cities.

Value Zone

FA

The rise of slums in most Indian cities is due to poverty and also a result of unplanned growth of cities.

Activity Zone

Find out about three more Indian cities and fill in the table.

City	State	Places to Visit	Food	Famous for

My Zone

FA

Draw a smiley 🙂 if you know and a star ⭐ if you wish to know more.

1. I know about more cities of India. ....
2. I know about the union territory, Chandigarh. ....
3. In know that each city has its own food habits, practices and tourist attractions. ....

Pin It Up

Find out about the islands of India. Write a short paragraph about each group of islands on a sheet of paper and pin it up.

13 Transport and Communication in India

I Know ...

- Farmers use a .... to carry wheat to the flour mill.
- The fastest means of communication is the ....

Observe and Reflect

- What do you see in the picture?
- How do camels help people in deserts?
- Why is this animal called the ship of the desert?

How do you go to school every day? Some of us take the school bus, some of us go by **carpool** and some of us walk to school. Vehicles that we use to move from one place to another are known as the means of **transport**. We use different types of vehicles to travel on land, water and by air. Let us learn more about them.

Land Transport

The vehicles that we use to travel on land are of two types: **road transport** and **rail transport**.

Cars, scooters, bikes and buses are means of road transport. These vehicles run on fuel. We use trucks to transport goods from one place to another. Some vehicles mostly found in villages or rural areas are bullock carts, bicycles and tractors. These are used for transporting both goods and people. In the desert region, people use camels. Elephants are also used for transportation in forest areas. Mules and ponies are used in hilly areas for transportation.

Trains and metro trains are means of rail transport. In cities like Mumbai, local trains are very important as a majority of the population depends on them to move around the city. In cities like Kolkata and Delhi, metro trains are more popular. Trains in India run on steam, diesel and electricity. In Kolkata, we can even find trams in some parts of the city.

Rail transport

FA

Do It Yourself

While crossing the roads or walking, it is important to stay safe so that no accidents happen. Tick (✓) the road safety rules that need to be followed and cross out (✗) the ones that can be avoided.

- Always walk on the **pavement**. ☐
- Use the zebra crossing to cross the road. ☐
- Cross the road without looking at both sides of the road. ☐
- Always obey traffic lights. ☐
- Use overbridges and subways for crossing roads. ☐
- Cross rail tracks even when the gates are closed. ☐

Water Transport

Water transport is the oldest means of transport. When we travel by water we use boats, ships and steamers. Rafts and submarines are also useful means of water transport. Canoes, kayaks and rafts are means of transport that are used in adventure sports.

Air Transport

Air transport takes the least amount of time since it can cover large distances in a really short time. Helicopters and aeroplanes are means of air transport.

Find Out

When was the first aeroplane invented and by whom?

Travelling Outside the Country

While travelling within a country, we require an identification card. However, when we travel to another country, we need some other documents. One such document is a **passport**. A passport shows that we are citizens of a country. To enter other countries, we require permission or a **visa**. A visa is a stamp on the passport that gives us the permission to enter other countries. These documents are checked at the airport.

Passport

Major Forms of Communication

You already know that communication means sending and receiving messages. In the beginning, pigeons were used to send messages. Men and animals also carried messages. However, these took a long time to reach. Communication now has become much quicker and easier due to better means of communication. Communication can be of two types—personal communication and mass communication. Post, telephone and now the Internet are the major means of personal communication. Let us discuss the means of personal communication in detail.

Letters are a popular form of communication. People buy postcards and inland letters from post offices. One can also use plain paper to write messages and send them using a stamped envelope. Buses, trains, aeroplanes and ships carry letters and parcels.

Fact Zone

There are 1,54,866 post offices in India.

Nowadays, people use a **courier** service or speed post for sending urgent letters. They take less time to reach.

Telephones are the quickest way through which we can get in touch with people in any part of the world. Cellular phones help us to stay in touch with others even when we are travelling. The short message service (SMS) is also used for sending messages. One can also use a **fax** machine to send written messages, photos or letters. They reach the receiver because they are connected via telephone lines.

Fact Zone

Alexander Graham Bell invented the telephone in 1875.

Computers today are regarded as the most important mode of communication. One can use email (electronic mail) for sending videos, pictures, letters and books to anyone, anywhere on the planet. The Internet helps us to send out emails. It also helps us get important information from all over the world, such as weather reports, news reports and other kinds of information.

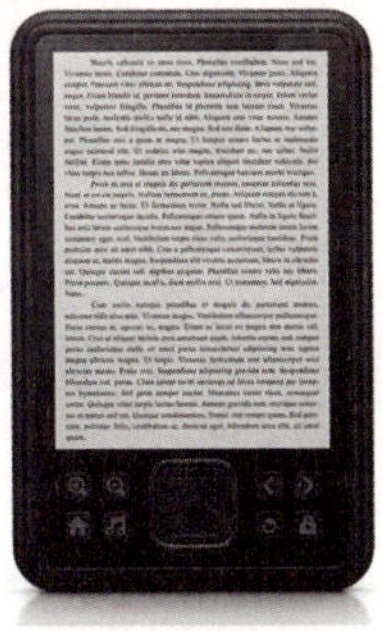

E-reader

E-readers and **tablets** also require the Internet to work. We can read books using these gadgets, listen to music, watch movies and also do most of the work that we can do on a computer.

What is Mass Communication?

Mass communication means communicating with many people at once. Newspapers, radio and television are the most common means of mass communication.

Eco Zone

Old newspapers can be reused for many purposes. Can you name a few?

Newspapers

Mass communication has now become quicker and easier because of satellites. They pick up television signals from different parts of the world and feed them to other parts of the world. This is why we are able to watch cricket matches when they are being played in another continent.

Remember

- We use different types of vehicles to travel on land, water and by air.
- Visas and passports are needed to travel outside our country.
- Telephones are the quickest mode of communication.
- Mass communication is a way of communication that helps us to get in touch with many people at the same time.

Words Zone

pavement: a flat, raised part at the side of a road for people to walk on

passport: an official document that identifies you as a citizen of a particular country

visa: a stamp on the passport granting permission to enter a particular country

courier: to send important papers or a package quickly

Review Zone

A Fill in the blanks with the correct answers.

1. Local trains are popular in ....
   a. Mumbai b. Kolkata c. Delhi
2. One can see trams in ....
   a. Kolkata b. Chennai c. Bengaluru
3. The Metro is an important mode of transport in ....
   a. Delhi b. Hyderabad c. Jaipur
4. We need to be connected to the .... line to send a document using the fax machine.
   a. Internet b. telephone c. television
5. A .... gives us the permission to enter another country.
   a. conductor b. visa c. school

B Unscramble the jumbled words to get some names of the different means of transport and communications. Take the letters in the circled box and unscramble them to get the final word.

1. TESALLEIT
2. SAIV
3. TEPNEOHEL
4. XAF
5. TIENNRET
6. PHIS
7. POANERLAE
8. SUB

Answer

C Answer these questions in brief.

1. What connection do we need to send an email?
2. How do people in villages transport goods?
3. What documents are required to travel outside a country?

4. What is mass communication?
5. Which electronic gadgets are used to read books?

D **Answer these questions in detail.**

1. What is the contribution of the Internet and the telephone in communication?
2. What are the different modes of transport?
3. Name the ways through which we can communicate with many people at the same time.

Think Zone

A What happens when we don't follow traffic rules?

B **Look at the picture and answer the questions.**

1. Identify the object in the picture.
2. How does it help in communication?

Life Skills Zone

We have already learned that vehicles let out smoke into the environment and pollute it. Make a list of four things that you can do to help clean the environment.

Value Zone

Offer old people your seat in buses and metros.

Activity Zone

FA

Make a hot air balloon

You will need sheets of colourful paper, thread and glue.

1. Take one sheet of colourful paper and cut it into the shape of a balloon.
2. Take the blue coloured papers and cut them into the shape of clouds. Paste the clouds and the balloon on to the white sheet as shown in the picture.

3. Now, take the thread and paste one end of it to the balloon along the clouds. Now, your balloon is flying above the clouds!

My Zone

FA

Draw a smiley if you know and a star if you wish to know more.

1. I know that there are three different modes of transport—land, water and air. ....
2. I know the different ways by which we travel in India. ....
3. I know the different ways by which people communicate in India. ....

Pin It Up

Paste a picture of your favourite mode of transport on a sheet of paper and write a few lines on why you like it.

14 Lifestyle in India

I Know ...

- Early humans learned to cook food when .... was discovered.
- Early man used to wear .... as clothes.

Observe and Reflect

- What is this dish called?
- Which city in India has its name added to the name of this dish?
- Do you know the story behind how this dish first came to be made?

We have learned about the different cities of India and also about the various means of transport and communication that are available in India. Now, we will learn about the variety of food that India offers and the different kinds of clothes that people wear.

Food

India is a very diverse country. Different types of food items are found in different regions. The climate, the type of soil, availability of water and location affect the type of food available in different regions.

Indian food is unique because of the various types of ingredients used to cook different dishes like spices, grains, pulses, vegetables, fruits and oilseeds.

In India, **food grains** are the main food for most of the people. Whole wheat, *bajra* (pearl millet), *jowar* (millet), rice and *makkai* (corn) are some of the important food grains of India. While the main food grain of eastern and southern India is rice,

Rice

Chapatti

wheat is the most common food grain in the northern states of India. *Bajra* and *jowar* are used often in the desert state of Rajasthan.

Mung beans, *urad* dal, garbanzo beans or chickpeas, *masoor* dal and *toor* dal (pigeon pea) are some of the main **pulses** in India.

Oilseeds such as mustard and sesame (*til*) are used to produce oil. People in the eastern states use mustard oil as the medium of cooking, whereas in the southern states coconut oil and *til* oil are used for cooking. People also use sunflower seed oil or rice bran oil. *Ghee* is often used in Punjab.

Fact Zone

Most of the states in India have their own sweet dish. Shrikhand is the sweet dish of Maharashtra.

Shopa/suwa (aniseed), *hing* (asafoetida), *mirch* (chilli/pepper), *elaichi* (cardamom), *kali mirch* (peppercorn) are some of the **spices** that are most commonly used in Indian dishes. Kerala is the land of spices. Indian food is generally spicy and its curries are famous worldwide.

Spices of India

In order to increase the taste of the dish, some **herbs** and leaves like basil, coriander, mint and curry leaves are used in Indian dishes.

All **fruits** and **vegetables** are not available throughout the year. Their availability varies from season to season. Potatoes, cabbages, carrots and brinjals are some of the most common vegetables of India. Mangoes, apples, oranges, coconuts and grapes are popular fruits in India.

Special Dishes

Let us learn about the special dishes of the different states of India. Each state is known for its food, which is absolutely different from other states. A few examples of the most famous foods of some states of India are given below:

Find Out

Which state does *gatte ki sabji* come from?

- Jammu and Kashmir - *Rogan josh*
- Rajasthan - *Dal baati choorma*
- Gujarat - *Dhokla*
- Telangana - Hyderabadi *biryani*
- Bihar/Jharkhand - *Thekua*
- Punjab - *Makke di roti*
- Uttar Pradesh - *Shami kebab*
- Maharashtra - *Vada pav*
- Tamil Nadu - *Dosa*
- West Bengal - *Bhapa ilish*

Though each state has its own special dish, the dishes are not made in those states only. People from different states enjoy the special dishes from other states and cook them as well. For example, Bengali food is available in Delhi and Gujarati *dhoklas* are found in Kolkata! Fruits and vegetables too are bought and sold from one state to another.

Eco Zone

We get food from plants and animals. If the environment is clean, then our food will also be clean and healthy.

Climate and Clothing

Just like dishes, people of different states of India wear different clothes. This is because different states have different climatic conditions. Indians wear different clothes on special occasions as well.

Do It Yourself

Can you name these outfits?

Just like each state has its own dish, each state also has its own clothing customs. These are called **traditional** dresses.

Saree: Women of different states wear sarees in different styles. This is a traditional dress that is worn by women across India.

Ghagra choli or *lehenga choli*: These colourful dresses are mainly worn by women of Gujarat and Rajasthan.

Salwaar kameez: North Indian women, especially Punjabis, wear salwaar kameez. It has, however, now become popular across India.

Reshme langa or *pattu pavadai*: These are dresses commonly worn in Rajasthan and south India.

Mekhela chador: This dress is a famous traditional dress of Assam.

In addition, women in cities also wear skirts, dresses, jeans, T-shirts, etc.

Now, let us take a look at some of the traditional Indian dresses for men:

Dhoti: This is worn by men in villages of warmer states. Dhoti is also a traditional Bengali dress for men, which they wear on special occasions.

Lungi: Men across India wear lungis.

Sherwani: Men from the north Indian states wear sherwanis on special occasions.

Pagri: People of Rajasthan and those who belong to the Sikh religion wear *pagris* or turbans.

Pheta caps: Men of Maharashtra, Karnataka and Rajasthan generally wear these. *Pheta* is a Marathi word, which means turban.

In addition, men in the cities generally wear jackets, T-shirts, shirts and trousers.

Find Out

Who introduced jeans in India?

Remember

- Different states have different and special food items.
- The clothing in different parts of India differs mainly on the basis of climatic conditions.

Words Zone

traditional: beliefs, customs or way of life of the people that has not changed for a long time

Review Zone

A **Fill in the blanks with the correct answers.**

1. .... is a herb.

   a. Basil b. Brasil c. Brazil

2. *Makke di roti* comes from ....

   a. Punjab b. Haryana c. Rajasthan

3. *Ghagra choli* is worn in ....

   a. Maharashtra b. Goa c. Rajasthan

4. Pearl millet is also known as .... in India.

   a. *bajra* b. *jowar* c. *makkai*

5. .... is from Bihar.

   a. *Mekna* b. *Sekna* c. *Thekua*

B **Write T for True and F for False.**

1. People who live in hot places in India like to wear cotton clothes. ☐
2. Indians do not wear special dresses on festive occasions. ☐
3. Food in India is not the same in every region. ☐
4. A carrot is a fruit. ☐
5. *Dhokla* comes from Gujarat. ☐

C **Answer these questions in brief.**

1. Which state is famous for *rogan josh*?
2. Name the factors affecting the type of food that is cooked in different states.
3. Name five types of traditional clothes that are worn in India.
4. Name four dishes that are made in various parts of India and write the state where these dishes are made.

D Answer these questions in detail.

1. What do you know about the clothes worn in different parts of India?
2. Write a short note on the different ingredients that are used in Indian cooking.
3. Name some of the special dishes from various states of India.
4. Why do different states have different variety of dishes?

Think Zone

FA

A Sometimes, we wear clothes of certain colours according to the season. Which colours would you pick for your clothes during each season?

B Look at the picture and answer the questions.

1. What outfits do you see in the picture?
2. On which occasions do people wear these clothes?

Life Skills Zone

Each state in India has some special dishes. Identify these food items from different Indian states.

....

....

Activity Zone

Form groups in your class and ask each group to dress up in any of the traditional dresses that you have learned about. Talk about the dress you are wearing and the state to which it belongs.

FA

Value Zone

Donate your old clothes to the poor.

FA

My Zone

Draw a smiley if you know and a star if you wish to know more.

1. I know that we get different types of food in India. ....
2. I know that people in India wear different clothes. ....
3. I know that we have special clothes that we wear only on special occasions. ....

Pin It Up

Take a picture of yourself wearing traditional clothes and pin it up.

15 Culture in India

I Know ...

- Holi is the festival of ....
- .... is the festival of lights.

Observe and Reflect

- Which national festival is shown in the picture?
- Can you name the place where this event takes place every year for the nation?
- In which city is it located?

India is a land of unity in diversity. We have already learned that there are 29 states and seven union territories. Each state has different beliefs, habits and ways of life. We celebrate different festivals. There are different types of dances and music that we enjoy. All these together form the **culture** of India.

Festivals of India

We celebrate three different kinds of festivals in India—religious, national and harvest festivals. Each festival that we celebrate in India has its own importance.

Fact Zone

Some festivals like Basant Panchami, Teej, Lohri and Sankranti are celebrated to mark the change of seasons.

Religious and National Festivals

We celebrate religious festivals on days that are special to a particular religion. The Hindus celebrate **Diwali**, Muslims celebrate **Eid**, Christians celebrate **Christmas** and Sikhs celebrate **Gurpurab**. On these festivals, we enjoy eating special food, we exchange gifts and we visit family and friends.

National festivals are the festivals that we celebrate together as a nation. These days are very special days for India. These festivals are **Independence Day**, **Republic Day** and **Gandhi Jayanti**. On these days, we have holidays and people of the entire country celebrate together.

Do It Yourself

Identify these festivals.

....

Harvest Festivals

People put in a lot of hard work to grow crops. During the harvest season, the crops become fully grown and are ready to be used. Harvest festivals, such as Baisakhi and Pongal are celebrated to express gratitude for the food that has been gathered. Given below are some of the major harvest festivals of India.

Magh Bihu in Assam is an important harvest festival that is celebrated during the months of January and February. People light up fires, eat good food and celebrate by performing Bihu, the traditional dance of Assam.

Pongal is celebrated in Tamil Nadu. During this time, a dish made of rice and jaggery is prepared and offered to the Sun, whom they **worship** as their god. This dish is called pongal and hence, the name of the festival is also pongal.

Onam is the harvest festival of Kerala. King Mahabali is worshipped on this day and people take part in boat races to celebrate this festival.

Holi is the most **popular** harvest festival that is celebrated throughout India. It is celebrated during

Eco Zone

During Holi and Lohri, people light bonfires, which harm the environment. Also, a lot of trees are cut down for firewood.

spring in order to mark a good harvest of crops like wheat, millet and mustard. People play with colours during this festival.

Dance Forms of India

The dance forms of India can be divided into two main forms—**classical** and **folk** dances.

The classical dance forms of India have existed for thousands of years and were performed mainly in temples and religious institutions or in front of kings and other important people. Each dance form comes from a particular state.

Bharatnatyam

- Bharatnatyam – Tamil Nadu
- Kathak – Uttar Pradesh
- Kathakali – Kerala
- Kuchipudi – Andhra Pradesh
- Manipuri – Manipur
- Mohiniyattam – Kerala
- Odissi – Odisha
- Sattriya – Assam

The folk dance forms of India are simpler dance forms. They are performed on special occasions to express happiness and joy. Some of them are mentioned below:

- Bihu and Chhau from eastern India
- Garbha and Raas from western India
- Padayani and Kummi from southern India
- Bhangra and Dumhal from northern India

Chhau dance

Indian Classical Music

Indian classical music can be divided into two types—**Hindustani** and **Carnatic**. Hindustani music is primarily practised in northern India and the main forms are *drupad* and *khyal*. Carnatic music is primarily practised in southern India. The musical instruments that are used in Indian classical music are tabla, santoor, veena, flute, shehnai, sitar, sarod, harmonium and tambura.

Find Out

Who is regarded as the greatest flute player of India?

Remember

- The festivals of India can be divided into harvest, religious and national festivals.
- The dance forms of India can be divided into classical and folk dance.
- Indian classical music can be divided into two types—the Hindustani classical music and the Carnatic music.

Words Zone

culture: ideas, customs and the way of life of a particular society

worship: showing respect for your God by saying prayers, singing, etc.

popular: liked or enjoyed by a large number of people

Review Zone

A Fill in the blanks with the correct answers.

1. Holi is a .... festival of India.

   a. religious b. national c. harvest

2. Bharatnatyam is a classical dance from ....

   a. Tamil Nadu b. Puducherry c. Sri Lanka

3. .... is celebrated on 15 August.

   a. Independence Day b. Republic Day c. Flag Day

4. Diwali is celebrated by ....

   a. lighting diyas b. throwing colours c. putting up Christmas trees

B Write T for True and F for False.

1. Classical dances were performed in front of common people. ☐
2. Chhau is a folk dance form of India. ☐
3. Carnatic music is practised in south India. ☐
4. Christmas is a national festival. ☐
5. Gandhi Jayanti is the birthday of Indira Gandhi. ☐

C Read the clues. Solve the crossword to name the different dance forms of India.

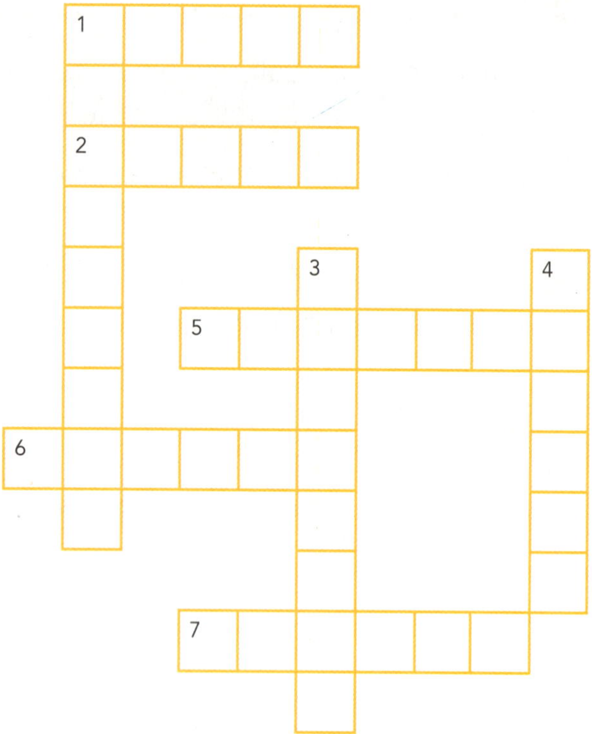

Across

1. Folk dance from south India
2. Folk dance from east India
5. Folk dance from the state of Punjab
6. Classical dance from the state of Odisha
7. Folk dance popular in the state of Gujarat

Down

1. Classical dance from the state of Andhra Pradesh
3. Classical dance from the state of Manipur
4. Classical dance from the state of Uttar Pradesh

D Answer these questions in brief.

1. Name any two religious festivals of India.
2. Name any two harvest festivals of India.
3. On which day do we celebrate Mahatma Gandhi's birthday?
4. Name two music forms of India.
5. Where did the Kuchipudi dance come from?

E Answer these questions in detail.

1. Write a short note on the different classical dance forms of India.
2. What is the difference between Hindustani classical and Carnatic music?
3. Name the harvest festivals of India.
4. Describe the three national festivals of India.

Think Zone

A How do you feel when you listen to your favourite song?

B **Look at the picture and answer the questions.**

1. Identify the famous musician in the picture.
2. Which musical instrument does he play?

FA

Life Skills Zone

Find out about western classical music. Learn about three instruments and three famous composers of western classical music.

FA

Value Zone

People from different parts of India have different customs. We should respect their customs and habits.

Activity Zone

Match the musical instruments to their names.

tabla   santoor   sitar   sarod   harmonium   tambura

 ....

 ....

 ....

 ....

 ....

 ....

FA

My Zone

Draw a smiley if you know and a star if you wish to know more.

1. I know that we celebrate different kinds of festivals in India. ....
2. I know that we have different kinds of dances in India. ....
3. I know that we have different types of music in India. ....

Pin It Up

Find out about any two harvest festivals celebrated in the world. Collect pictures and paste them on a sheet of paper.

Assessment 3 (Chapters 11-15)

Maximum Marks: 25

Ⓐ Fill in the blanks. (1 x 8 = 8)

1. The Kamakhya Temple is located in the city of ....
2. The Marina Beach ends at the .... Beach.
3. Jaipur is also known as the ....
4. *Lehenga choli* is a dress worn by women of ....
5. Magh Bihu is a .... festival of Assam.
6. The .... is the traditional dress of Assam.
7. .... is the land of spices.
8. The main food grain of West Bengal is ....

Ⓑ Match the columns. (1 x 10 = 10)

Column A	Column B
1. *Makke di roti*	a. Chennai
2. Kannada	b. Hyderabad
3. Statues made from waste material	c. *Chikankari*
4. A kind of fuel on which cars run	d. Bengaluru
5. Guindy	e. *Pheta*
6. Permission to enter another country	f. Punjab
7. A kind of embroidery	g. Snake
8. Pongal	h. Visa
9. A kind of headgear worn by people of Maharashtra	i. Chandigarh
10. Mecca Masjid	j. Diesel

Ⓒ Tick (✓) the appropriate answer. (1 x 7 = 7)

1. The city of Chennai developed around which of these forts?
   a. Fort William   b. Fort St George
2. What is Bengaluru famous for?
   a. Automobile industry   b. IT industry
3. What type of museum does Ahmedabad have?
   a. Kite museum   b. Rock museum
4. Which of these require Internet to work?
   a. Cellular phone   b. E-reader
5. Which of these is a classical dance form?
   a. Kathakali   b. Asteroids
6. Which of these is celebrated in Kerala?
   a. Onam   b. Pongal
7. Which of these originated in Uttar Pradesh?
   a. Kathak   b. Kuchipudi

16 Occupations in India

I Know ...

- People who grow crops are called ....
- Cotton clothes are made from the ....

Observe and Reflect

- What are the people in the picture doing?
- Do you know what they do for a living?
- How does their work benefit us?

Have you ever wondered why our parents go to work or office every day? All the people we see around us do some kind of work. Shopkeepers open their shops every day and sell goods. Farmers work in the fields in order to harvest crops. The work that people do from which they earn their living is known as an **occupation**. Now, we will learn about the different types of occupations practised by the people of India.

Agriculture is the most important occupation in India especially in villages and small towns. Farmers grow food crops and other crops. Farmers also **domesticate** animals like poultry and cattle for their meat, milk, eggs and other products. Some farmers grow cotton, tea, coffee and jute. These are called **raw materials**. After the farmer has grown the crops, these raw materials go to various **industries** where they are made into **manufactured** goods.

Find Out

Where in India do farmers grow crops like rice?

Besides agriculture and industries, people in India also take up other occupations that do not require a lot of physical work. For example, people work in banks, post offices, telephone offices, restaurants and hospitals. These places provide us with **services** in our everyday lives. Most of these service-based occupations are common in cities.

> **Fact Zone**
>
> Punjab and Haryana are the largest wheat producing states in India.

How Flour Reaches Us

We buy food from shops and the market but how does the food get there? Let us see how flour reaches us in the form of roti.

Farmers grow crops for us. They sow the seeds first and then **cultivate** the crop. When the plants grow, farmers cut the crops and gather them. This is called **harvesting**. When the wheat, which is the raw material, is ready, it is packed and taken to a **flour mill**. Here, the wheat is made into flour with the help of machines. Then this ready flour is packed, sent to shops and finally we buy the flour from there. In India, flour is also made from rice, gram, chickpea, bajra, maize and corn.

Flour made into roti

A farmer growing wheat

Harvested wheat being transported to the market

Wheat ground into flour

Flour being sold in shops

How Clothes are Made

We wear *kurtas* of various designs, shapes and colours. We know that *kurtas* are made from cloth, but where does the cloth come from?

Farmers grow the cotton plant in fields. The cotton that is plucked from the plants is the raw material. It is then taken to factories where people spin it into thread. The people who spin cotton into thread are called **spinners**. The threads are then taken to factories where **weavers** weave the thread into cloth. When the cloth is ready, tailors stitch beautiful kurtas from this cloth.

> **Eco Zone**
>
> Too much farming on a piece of land decreases the quality of the soil.

> **Find Out**
>
> Which raw material is used to make paper?

A team of people work together to produce these manufactured goods. Therefore, these occupations involve teamwork.

A farmer plucking cotton from cotton plants

A spinner spinning cotton into thread

A weaver weaving cloth in a loom

A tailor stitching clothes from the cloth

Do It Yourself

Label the raw materials shown below R and the manufactured goods as M.

....

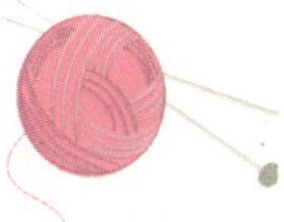

....

....

....

....

....

....

....

Arts and Crafts in India

India is well known for its arts and crafts. **Artisans** use different raw materials and different designs to make many beautiful objects.

Goods made in especially Rajasthan, Punjab, Uttar Pradesh, Gujarat, Assam and south India are famous around the world.

Embroidered cloth

Juttis

Silk

Bamboo goods

Madhubani paintings

Marble inlay work

Remember

- The work that people do in order to earn their living is known as an occupation.
- The jobs done in India can be divided into agriculture, industry and services.
- The conversion of wheat into flour is an example of how an agricultural raw material is made into a manufactured product.
- India is well-known for its art and craft and each region in India has its speciality.

Words Zone

manufactured: processed into a product

cultivate: to grow crops

flour mill: a mill used to grind wheat into flour

artisan: a person who makes things with his or her hands; a craftsman

domesticate: to make animals help humans for work

Review Zone

A Fill in the blanks with the correct answers.

1. .... turn threads into cloth.

   a. Spinners b. Weavers c. Farmers

2. When the wheat crops ripen, the farmers .... them.

   a. sow b. harvest c. plant

3. Banking is a/an .... job.

   a. agricultural b. service c. industrial

4. .... is the product manufactured from wheat.

   a. Corn b. Rubber c. Flour

B Write T for True and F for False.

1. The cultivation of crops like coffee cannot be regarded as agriculture. ☐
2. Raw materials from agriculture are used by industries. ☐
3. Telephone offices are a part of the industrial sector. ☐
4. Cultivated wheat is sold by farmers directly in the market. ☐
5. The arts and crafts of India are well known around the world. ☐

C Answer these questions in brief.

1. Which is the main occupation in India?
2. What are raw materials?
3. Which raw materials are used to make flour?
4. Which raw materials are used to make clothes?
5. Name two arts and crafts that India is famous for.

D Answer these questions in detail.

1. Write a short note on the work farmers do.
2. Describe how wheat flour reaches cities.
3. How is a *kurta* made from cotton?
4. What do you know about the arts and crafts of India?

Think Zone

A Spinners and weavers have always had an important role in India.

However, with the coming of modern industries, do you think they continue to play an important role?

B **Look at the picture and answer the questions.**

1. Identify the object in the picture.
2. What is it used for?
3. Who uses this machine?

Life Skills Zone

Find out how craftsmen and artisans are treated by the people who sell their goods. Do they get enough money for the amount of work that they do?

Value Zone

FA

We should treat people who provide things and services to us with kindness and respect.

Activity Zone

FA

Find out how sugar is made from sugarcane. How is it different from the process of making flour from wheat? Write the steps in your notebook.

My Zone

FA

Draw a smiley if you know and a star if you wish to know more.

1. I know that there are three different types of occupations in India. ....
2. I know that there are different stages through which a manufactured product goes through. ....
3. I know that there are different types of artisans and craftsmen who make beautiful objects. ....

Pin It Up

Prepare a collage on Indian handicrafts. Collect pictures of different kinds of arts and crafts made in India and paste it on a drawing sheet.

17 Famous Indians

I Know ...

- Gandhi Jayanti is celebrated on ....
- Dr Radhakrishnan was the second .... of India.

Observe and Reflect

- Who do you see in the picture?
- Which country is he from?
- What are the people of this country called?

A country does not become great by itself. It is the people living in a country that make it great. Until now, we have learned about the different festivals, the important cities, the variety of food and clothes, the different types of music and dance forms, and the various habits and customs of the people of India. Now, we will learn about some of India's most important people who have helped in making the country what it is today.

Maharana Pratap

Maharana Pratap, one of the bravest Rajput kings in India's history, ruled Mewar from 1572 till 1597. He was the eldest son of Udai Singh, the **founder** of Udaipur.

Maharana Pratap

He was the only Rajput king who refused to bow down to Emperor Akbar. When Akbar finally went to war against Mewar,

Maharana Pratap fought bravely in the battle. Although the Rajputs were defeated, he did not stop and continued his war against Emperor Akbar. Even today, Maharana Pratap is remembered as a great **warrior** and a king who loved his people and protected them until his death.

Rabindranath Tagore

Rabindranath Tagore was a great poet, writer and artist. He was born in Kolkata in 1861. He wrote the national **anthem** of India. Tagore was the first Indian to win the Nobel Prize for his book of poems called *Gitanjali*. Tagore also wrote a lot of songs known as *Rabindra Sangeet*. Even now people enjoy the dance dramas and plays written by him. Mahatma Gandhi called him 'Gurudev', which means a great teacher.

Find Out

Apart from India, which other country has its national anthem composed by Rabindranath Tagore?

Fact Zone

Rabindranath Tagore wrote his first poem when he was 8 years old.

Mahatma Gandhi

Mahatma Gandhi is also known as the Father of the Nation. He was born in Gujarat on 2 October 1869. Which national festival is celebrated on this day?

Mahatma Gandhi

Mahatma Gandhi was an important freedom fighter and one of the greatest leaders of India. During the freedom struggle, he led the people of India to freedom and believed in *ahimsa* or non-violence. He taught people that independence can be gained through peaceful means. He also taught people that every job is special and equal. He was lovingly called *Bapu* by the people.

Mother Teresa

Mother Teresa came to Kolkata at the age of 19 to become a teacher in a girls' school. However, in Calcutta she saw how the sick and the poor lived, and wanted to help them. Soon, this became her work and she did it for the rest of her life. Mother Teresa cared for street children, homeless children and old people.

Mother Teresa

She started Nirmal Hriday, a home for the sick and dying. Her **selfless dedication** and devotion towards Indians made her a true Indian. She was awarded the Noble Peace Prize in 1979.

She also received the Bharat Ratna, which is the highest award that can be given to an Indian.

Dr Sarvapalli Radhakrishnan

Dr Sarvapalli Radhakrishnan was born on 5 September 1888 in Andhra Pradesh. He was a great teacher. Radhakrishnan believed that all Indians are equal. He was the first vice president of India. He also wrote a number of books from which people around the world learned about India. Each year, his birthday is celebrated as Teachers' Day.

Radhakrishnan's student once went to him and wanted to celebrate his birthday. He told his students that instead of celebrating his birthday, they should celebrate teachers all over the country for the wonderful work they are doing. That was the first Teacher's Day celebrated in the country. Since then, schools and students celebrate this day to show that they are thankful to their teachers.

Dr Sarvapalli Radhakrishnan

FA

Do It Yourself

Name a famous Indian from each of these fields.

Art .... Music ....

Film .... Dance ....

Sports .... Writer ....

Remember

- Maharana Pratap is remembered as a great warrior and as the king who loved his people and has protected them until his death.
- Mahatma Gandhi is also known as the Father of the Nation.
- Mother Teresa selflessly served the poor, sick and needy people.

Words Zone

founder: a person who starts an organization or institution, or causes something to be built

warrior: a person who fights in a battle or war

anthem: a song that has a special importance for a country

- Dr Sarvapalli Radhakrishnan's birthday is celebrated as Teacher's Day each year.

selfless: thinking more about the happiness of others

dedication: the hard work and effort that somebody puts into an activity

Review Zone

A **Fill in the blanks with the correct answers.**

1. Rabindranath Tagore was born in ....
   a. 1861 b. 1862 c. 1863
2. Mahatma Gandhi was born on .... October.
   a. 2 b. 3 c. 4
3. Mother Teresa was born in ....
   a. 1910 b. 1911 c. 1912
4. Dr Sarvapalli Radhakrishnan was born in ....
   a. 1888 b. 1889 c. 1887
5. Tagore wrote his first poem when he was .... years old.
   a. 8 b. 9 c. 7

B **Match the columns.**

Column A	Column B
1. Mahatma Gandhi	a. Nirmal Hriday
2. Mother Teresa	b. Mewar
3. Dr Radhakrishnan	c. *Gitanjali*
4. Tagore	d. First vice president of India
5. Maharana Pratap	e. *Ahimsa*

C **Write T for True and F for False.**

1. Mahatma Gandhi believed in non-violence.
2. Mother Teresa did not care about the conditions of the sick and the poor.
3. Dr Radhakrishnan's birthday is celebrated as Teacher's Day each year.
4. Tagore never won the Nobel Prize.
5. Mother Teresa was born in India.

D **Answer these questions in brief.**

1. Who was Rabindranath Tagore?
2. What did Mahatma Gandhi believe in?
3. How old was Mother Teresa when she came to India?
4. Who wrote the national anthem of India?

E **Answer these questions in detail.**

1. How is Maharana Pratap remembered today?
2. Write a few lines about Dr Radhakrishnan.
3. What did Mother Teresa do in India?

Think Zone

FA

A **Circle the qualities you think are required to make a great leader.**

ambition	kindness	jealousy	trustworthy
loyalty	greed	responsibility	respect

B **Look at the picture and answer the questions.**

1. Who do you see in this picture?
2. What does he do?
3. Does he help in making the country a better place to live?

Life Skills Zone

There are many people who help the poor without expecting anything in return. They teach, they donate and they spend their time caring for others. Find out about one such person and write a few lines about the work he or she does. Do you also wish to do these things?

Value Zone

We must always try to help others when they need it.

Activity Zone

FA

Collect pictures and information about the Armed Forces in India. Write how they help us.

My Zone

FA

Draw a smiley 🙂 if you know and a star ⭐ if you wish to know more.

1. I know that there are many people who have worked hard towards making India a better nation. ....
2. I know about a few Indians who have contributed in making this nation successful. ....

Pin It Up

Name the Indian whom you admire the most. Write his or her name and in one paragraph explain why he or she is famous. You can even paste his or her photograph.

18 Understanding the Past

I Know ...

- When my grandparents were young, they .... (had/did not have) mobile phones.
- My parents .... (played/did not play) video games when they were small.

Observe and Reflect

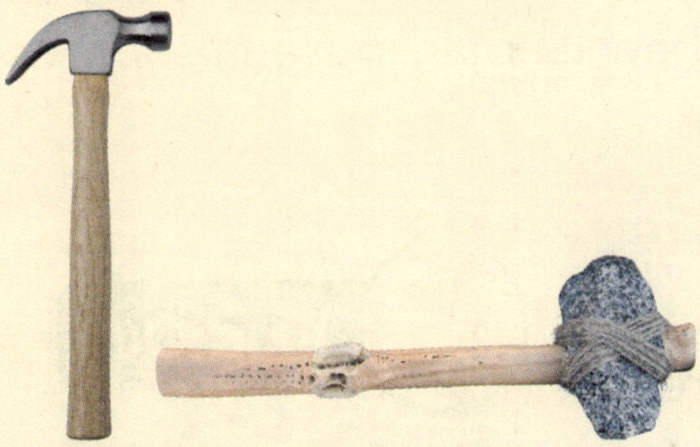

- What are these two objects?
- Can they both do the same kind of work?
- Are they made with the same materials?

What is History?

We know that things were different during our grandparents' time from what they are today. How do we learn about them? We learn about our grandparents' time by observing the pictures and the things they used when they were our age, and comparing those things with the things that we use today. Things that happened in the **past** are called **history**.

History tells us about the important events of the past. It also tells us about many important people in the past and what they did, the things they used and the food they ate.

How do we know about people who lived thousands of years ago? We observe the things that they used. These things are called sources of history.

Sources of History

Human beings have lived on the Earth for millions of years. Throughout the years, people have found things that human beings used during that time and have studied them.

Fact Zone

People who study the things that human beings used in the past are called archaeologists.

The remains of tools, coins, old pots, monuments, **inscriptions**, documents and cave paintings used and made by human beings in the past give us clues about how they lived, ate, worked and played. Skeletons and **fossils** of early humans have been found and studied by archaeologists. All these things have been kept in **museums**. Let us learn more about the sources of history.

Coins

From a coin we can understand what metals were used at that time and how skilled the people were. The inscriptions on the coins tell us about the time in which they were made.

Find Out

Name an animal that lived thousands of years ago.

Documents

Documents or written texts can be described as the best source of history because they give you direct information about people and events of the past. We learn about the people who lived during that time, the material that was used for writing and we learn about the things that happened during that period.

Monuments

With monuments, we get an idea of the style of **architecture** followed in a certain period and how the people lived. In certain monuments we find poems written in praise of famous rulers.

Eco Zone

People did not use vehicles in the past. Do you think the air was cleaner at that time?

Tools

Tools are especially helpful for people who are studying the past. They help us understand how early humans evolved to become what they are today.

Paintings

Paintings are an important source of information since many stories are told through them. They give an idea of the daily life and practices of the people in the past.

Timelines

Timelines are an extremely important source of history since they give us the exact dates of various events that happened in the past. For example, a timeline of the Mughal Empire will show us when it started and when it ended, which ruler ruled till which year and which important event took place in which year.

A timeline about your past will show you the year you were born in and in which year all the important events of your life happened, such as, the year you started walking, the year you started talking, the year you started going to school and so on. Timelines are helpful since they help us in understanding the order of important events in the past.

FA

Do It Yourself

Make a timeline of important events of your life. Write the event that happened at the top end of the line and the year it happened in at the bottom end of the line.

What happened

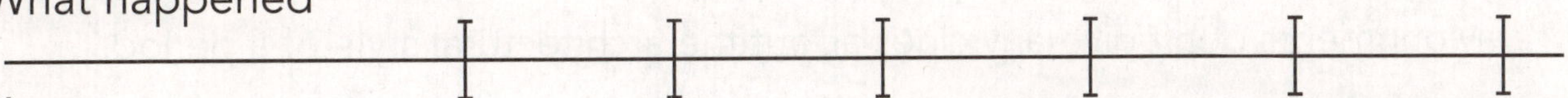

Year

Remember

» History is the study of the events of the past.

Words Zone

past: belonging to an earlier time

- Coins, documents, monuments, tools, cave paintings are important sources of history.
- Timelines give us definite dates and are, thus, very important in understanding history.

inscriptions: words written on the cover of a book or cut in stone or metal

fossil: remains of humans, animals, birds and plants

museum: a place where things from the past are kept

architecture: method or process of making a building

Review Zone

A Fill in the blanks with the correct answers.

1. .... have poems about many rulers inscribed on them.
   a. Pots b. Monuments c. Coins
2. .... give us an idea of the daily life and practices of the people.
   a. Coins b. Paintings c. Tools
3. The .... on coins also tell us about the time in which they were made.
   a. inscriptions b. paintings c. documents
4. .... give us the exact dates of various events that happened in the past.
   a. Documents b. Timelines c. Paintings

B Write T for True and F for False.

1. Monuments don't give any clues about the architectural style of a period. ☐
2. Paintings help us to learn more about the daily activities of the people of that time. ☐
3. Timelines give us an idea of dates of important events that happened in the past. ☐
4. Photographs can never be a source of history. ☐
5. Coins provide us direct information about history. ☐

C **Answer these questions in brief.**

1. What are timelines?
2. What is history?
3. What do we learn from cave paintings?
4. What information do coins give us?

D **Answer these questions in detail.**

1. How are timelines an important source of history?
2. Why is studying history important?
3. Write a short note on written documents as a source of history.
4. How do monuments help us learn about the past?

Think Zone

A How different would things have been if we did not know about the past?

B **Look at the picture and answer the questions.**

1. What do you see in the picture?
2. Would you say this picture shows the past?
3. Do people still dress this way today?

Life Skills Zone

Make a list of the games that your grandparents used to play. Did they watch TV or play video games? What did they use to send messages? How did they travel from place to place? Write a few lines on it and present it in class.

Value Zone

We should keep old things like photographs and cards carefully.

Activity Zone

FA

Do you believe that family albums are an important source of history about your family? Make an album of all the old photographs that you can collect and show how things used then are different from the things that we use today.

My Zone

FA

Draw a smiley if you know and a star if you wish to know more.

1. I know things that happened in the past are called history. ....
2. I know about the different sources of history. ....
3. I know that timelines give us the exact dates of important events. ....

Pin It Up

Look at any one of the cave paintings on the Internet. Write three sentences describing it.

19 Life of the Early Humans

I Know ...

- .... is the study of the past.
- Timelines tell us the exact .... of when events happened.

Observe and Reflect

- What are these type of paintings called?
- Who made such paintings?
- What does it show?

Early humans who lived on Earth millions of years ago were very different from us. Nowadays, we live in our own houses and cook our food on gas stoves or in microwaves. But, early humans did not enjoy these things. Have you ever wondered what kind of dresses they wore and where they lived? In this chapter, we will learn about them and their lives.

Fact Zone

Early humans can be called nomads or wanderers for they did not have a permanent home.

Hunter-gatherers

Early humans did not know the use of fire or how to farm and grow food. They mostly ate fruits, roots and berries that they gathered and they also hunted animals for their meat. Hence, early humans are known as **hunter-gatherers**.

Early humans had no fixed place that they called home. They moved from one place to another in search of food.

Shelter and Clothing

Early human beings did not know how to weave. So, they used barks and leaves to cover their bodies. They soon learned that the fur and skin of animals that they hunted could keep them warm at night.

Early humans lived in caves and other natural shelters like trees and **groves** to keep themselves protected from the cold, rain and wild animals.

Early humans were hunter-gatherers

Tools

Early humans made tools from materials like wooden sticks and stones. They used simple stone pieces with sharp edges to dig the ground for roots. Sharper tools were better for hunting. So, they tied them to long wooden sticks. They used these **spears** to hunt animals from a distance. Early humans also made tools from wood and bones.

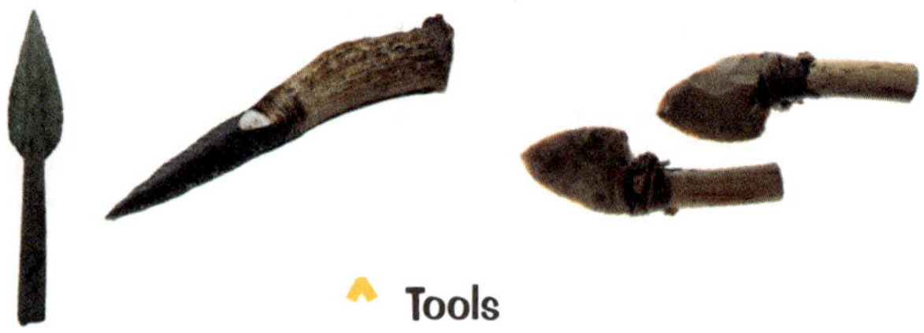

Tools

Fact Zone

As most of the tools were made from stone, this time period is also called the **Stone Age**.

Language and Art

Early humans used simple signs and hand movements to talk to one another. Later they started using sounds to communicate with each other.

Cave paintings have been found in a number of **sites** all over the world. These show animals and scenes of hunting.

From Hunter-gatherers to Settlers

We know that early humans gathered fruits and berries. When they threw away the seeds of these fruits, they found that the seeds grew into new

Eco Zone

Would you say that the Earth was greener during the time of the early humans?

plants. Thus, they discovered that plants grow from seeds. Soon, they started scattering seeds on a patch of land to grow food. Thus, began the story of farming.

They saw that the plants grew better after it rained. So, they realized that water helped the plants to grow faster. They started staying close to rivers and lakes.

Find Out

Name the settlements that developed along riverbanks.

As early humans learned to farm, they needed to stay in one place for a longer period of time as plants required time to grow.

Humans began to build huts with branches of trees, leaves, animal skins and stones. Later, they learned to make mud huts. Humans began to settle down in **communities** and villages.

They started to **domesticate** animals because animals could help them in their work. Animals like dogs were used to help them in hunting, while cows, goats, sheep and buffaloes were raised for their meat and other products. Animals like donkeys were also used as a means of transport.

FA

Do It Yourself

Plant your own vegetables.

1. Take some mustard seeds and put them in a pot with soil. Water the mustard seeds every morning and make sure it gets enough sunlight.
2. Keep a diary and note down how much the plant has grown in a week's time.
3. See how fast the seeds start sprouting into plants!

Remember

- Early humans were hunter-gatherers and moved from one place to another in search of food.
- Early humans made tools from stones, wood and bones.
- Early humans began to settle in one place in communities as they learned to farm.

Words Zone

groves: a small group of trees

spear: a weapon with a long wooden handle and a sharp metal point used for fighting, hunting and fishing in the past

site: a place where something is located

community: a group of people who live together

domesticate: to make a wild animal live and work for humans

Review Zone

A Fill in the blanks with the correct answers.

1. Early humans mostly ate fruits, roots, berries that they ....
   a. cooked b. gathered c. planted
2. Early humans had no permanent ....
   a. school b. home c. tent
3. Early humans took shelter in .... against wild animals.
   a. caves b. tents c. bushes
4. Early humans made .... from stones, wood and bones.
   a. food b. clothes c. tools

B Write T for True and F for False.

1. Early humans wandered from place to place. ☐
2. Early humans became settlers from hunter-gatherers. ☐
3. Early humans made tools from bones and wood. ☐

4. Early humans learned to grow crops from seeds. ☐

5. Early humans mainly used cows as a means of transport. ☐

C **Answer these questions in brief.**

1. What did early humans eat?
2. From what did the early humans make their clothes?
3. Why did early humans begin to stay in one place?
4. What kinds of animals helped early humans in their work?

D **Answer these questions in detail.**

1. Why are early humans also known as hunter-gatherers?
2. Describe how the earliest tools were made from stone and wood. How were these tools used?

Think Zone

A What do you think early humans did for fun?

B **Look at the picture and answer the questions.**

1. What is shown in the picture?
2. Which animals did the early humans domesticate?

Life Skills Zone

Early humans lived a nomadic life, which means they travelled from one place to another in search of food and shelter. There were no modern means of transportation in those days. They walked or used rafts and simple carts. What dangers and difficulties do you think they might have faced in their wanderings?

Value Zone

Like nomads, there are homeless people even today. They have no home and, sometimes, no food to eat. We should try to help them in any way we can.

Activity Zone

Make your own cave painting.

1. Take a brown sheet of paper or an old paper bag. Crumple it into a ball and then open it. You will see that it looks like the wall of a cave.

2. Then, draw your favourite animal on it. Don't use paint brushes or colour pencils. Instead, finger paint it. Dip your fingers in paint and then run them on the brown paper.

   You now have your own cave painting!

My Zone

Draw a smiley if you know and a star if you wish to know more.

1. I know that early humans were hunter-gatherers and moved from one place to another in search of food. ....
2. I know that early humans made tools from stones, wood and bones. ....
3. I know that early humans began to settle in one place in communities as they learned to farm. ....

Pin It Up

List any three difficulties early man might have faced in his life on a sheet of paper.

20 Fire and Wheel

I Know ...

- .... can be eaten without being cooked.
- Cars and other vehicles have .... (square/round/triangle) shaped wheels.

Observe and Reflect

- What do you see in the picture?
- What shape is it?
- What do we use it for?

Discovery of Fire

Early humans knew about fire as they would often see forest fires or when **lightning** struck trees. However, they were afraid of fire as they did not know how to control it. Early humans sharpened their stone tools by rubbing them together. In doing so, they might have found that fire could be created by rubbing two dry stones with each other.

Fire was useful to early humans in many different ways:

- Fire kept early humans warm in the bitter cold.

Eco Zone

If a fire breaks out in the forest, it causes forest fires. Forest fires are bad for the environment as well as for the people, animals and plants that live around it.

- Animals were afraid of fire. Early humans found that by lighting fire in front of their caves or shelters, wild animals used to run away.
- They discovered that meat, when roasted in fire, tasted better and softer. This is how humans learned to cook their food as well.

Early human striking two stones to make fire

Wheel

During the Stone Age, there were no cars or buses or trains that the early human could use to travel from one place to another. Early humans walked from one place to another and carried loads on their backs. This was a slow and difficult process. How do you think they travelled long distances?

Raft made from logs

They felt the need for easier ways of travelling. One of the earliest modes of transport was the **raft** made from logs of wood. Early humans saw logs floating on the water and began to tie them together to create rafts. However, they could not carry their load easily across rivers in these rafts.

Next, early humans built wooden carts or **sledges** to drag load from one place to another. They discovered that round logs, when fitted to these carts, made it easier to drag them over land. Thus, early humans discovered the wheel.

Wheels were useful as they made travelling faster. Early humans no longer had to walk over long distances.

- Early humans could carry loads easily.
- Wheels were useful in making clay pots and pans. The wheel used for this purpose was called a potter's wheel.

Fact Zone

Wheels on modern cars and other things have axles. An axle is a pole that runs through the wheel and around which the wheel turns.

Do It Yourself

How do you think early man invented the wheel? Number the pictures in the correct sequence.

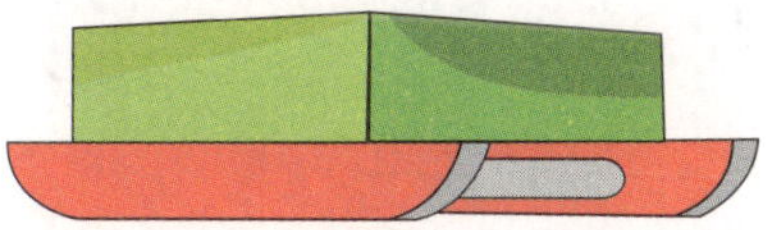

Remember

- The discovery of fire and the invention of the wheel made human lives easier and safer.
- Fire was used to keep warm, drive animals away and cook food.
- Wheels made travelling faster and safer.
- The earliest transport systems invented were rafts, carts and sledges.
- A potter's wheel was used to make clay pots and pans.

Words Zone

lightning: flashes of bright light seen in the sky

raft: a flat structure made of pieces of wood tied together and used as a boat invention

sledge: a vehicle used for travelling on snow and ice

invention: something that has been built for the first time

Review Zone

A **Fill in the blanks with the correct answers.**

1. Humans ate their food .... before the discovery of fire.
   a. cooked   b. rotten   c. raw
2. Animals and early humans were afraid of ....
   a. water   b. fire   c. fruits
3. Early humans used .... rafts to travel on water.
   a. stone   b. wooden   c. clay
4. .... was used to make pots.
   a. Bone   b. Clay   c. Stone

B **Tick (✓) the odd one out.**

1. dish	☐	pots	☐	jars	☐	knives	☐
2. meat	☐	fish	☐	mango	☐	egg	☐

C **Write T for True and F for False.**

1. Fire could be created by rubbing two wet stones together. ☐
2. Early humans used logs of wood to make rafts. ☐
3. Square wheels made it easier to drag carts over land. ☐
4. Long distance travel became easy after the wheel was invented. ☐

D **Answer these questions in brief.**

1. How did early humans use fire to make their food?
2. In the beginning, why were early humans afraid of fire?
3. What was the potter's wheel used for?
4. Which was one of the earliest means of transport?

E **Answer these questions in detail.**

1. How did the invention of fire make life easier for early man?
2. What are the uses of the wheel?

Think Zone

A Find out why animals were afraid of fire.

B **Look at the picture and list three ways in which fire is shown to be useful here.**

Life Skills Zone

Fire was an important discovery and the wheel was a necessary invention. What do you think is the difference between a discovery and an invention? Find out with the help of your teacher.

Value Zone

We should value old things from our grandparents', time. These things are not available to us anymore.

Activity Zone

Make an ice cream stick raft!

Collect ice cream sticks and place them on a surface one after the other. Take four more and paste them to the ice cream sticks vertically as shown in the picture. You have an ice cream stick raft ready!

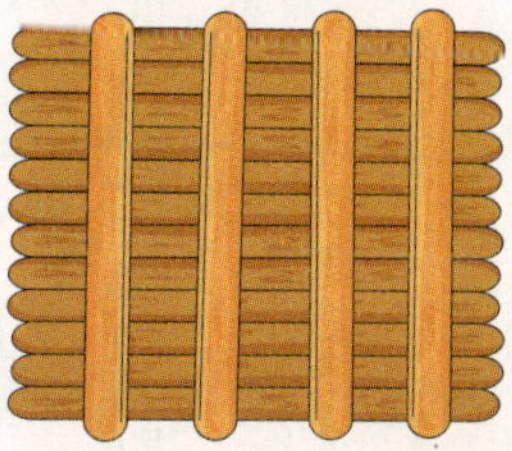

My Zone

Draw a smiley if you know and a star if you wish to know more.

1. I know that the discovery of fire and the invention of the wheel made early human's life better. ....
2. I know that after these discoveries, early humans could eat cooked food and travel easily. ....
3. I know that there are many uses of a wheel. ....

Pin It Up

Write a few lines on what you think life would have been like if early man had not discovered fire.

Assessment 4 (Chapters 16-20)

Maximum Marks: 25

A Fill in the blanks. (1 x 8 = 8)

1. Udai Singh founded the city of ....
2. Early humans raised goats and sheep for their ....
3. Potters use a .... to make clay pots.
4. Mother Teresa opened Nirmal Hriday for the .... and ....
5. The first vehicle used by early humans to travel is the ....
6. A .... is a source of history.
7. Cotton cloth is made from the .... plant.

B Match the columns. (1 x 10 = 10)

Column A	Column B
1. *Gitanjali*	a. Mahatma Gandhi
2. It gives us the exact dates of events	b. Sledge
3. Dogs helped early humans in this process	c. Inscription
4. Celebration of Teacher's Day	d. History
5. Used by early humans to keep animals away	e. Rabindranath Tagore
6. Non-violence	f. Sources
7. Source of history	g. Hunting
8. Transport used by early humans to drag loads	h. Fire
9. Clues that help us understand the past	i. Sarvapalli Radhakrishnan
10. Study of past events	j. Timeline

C Tick (✓) the appropriate answer. (1 x 7 = 7)

1. Where did early humans live?
   a. Caves   b. Mud huts
2. What were early humans called?
   a. Farmer-hunters   b. Hunter-gatherers
3. Where do we keep fossils?
   a. Museum   b. Home
4. Which one of these is an award given by the Indian government?
   a. Nobel Prize   b. Bharat Ratna
5. Which of these may be called a raw material?
   a. Cotton plant   b. Paper
6. Which of these is a herb?
   a. Mint   b. Cabbage
7. Which of these is a musical instrument?
   a. Sitar   b. Fax machine

Let's recycle! Learn how to make your own handmade paper.

You will need old paper scraps, a wire mesh, a pencil box and dried flowers.

1

Collect scraps of used paper and cut them into pieces.

2

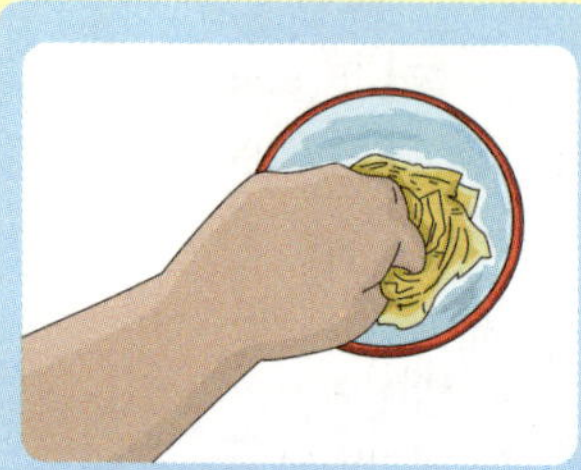

Once the pieces are cut, soak them in a bowl of water over night.

3

Next morning, you will see that the paper has turned into a gooey paste. Take this paste and with the help of an adult, grind it in a mortar and pestle or in a blender.

4

Once ground, take the mesh and start placing the paste over it.

5

Keep pressing it so that the water from the paste goes down the mesh. Make sure you press the paste down with a flat surface like a pencil box.

6

Take some dried flowers and place them on the wet surface of the paste.

7

Leave it to dry for the night.

8

In the morning, you will find that your handmade paper is ready!

Comprehensive Assessment 2 (Chapters 11-20) **Maximum Marks: 50**

A Tick (✓) the correct option. **(1 x 10 = 10)**

1. Which of these is not a spice?
   a. *Mung* b. *Mirch*
2. Which of these is not a food item from West Bengal?
   a. *Rogan josh* b. *Bhapa ilish*
3. Sattriya is the dance form of which state?
   a. Manipur b. Assam
4. Which of these is not a traditional dress worn by Indian women?
   a. Saree b. Sherwani
5. Which of these is a form of Hindustani classical music?
   a. Mohiniyattam b. Drupad
6. Which of these is a manufactured good?
   a. Cotton plant b. Saree
7. Which is a means of mass communication?
   a. Newspaper b. Telephone
8. Who was the ruler of Mewar?
   a. Akbar b. Pratap
9. Which of these was established by Mother Teresa?
   a. Sabarmati Ashram b. Nirmal Hriday
10. Which was the other name used to call Rabindranath Tagore?
    a. Gurudev b. Mahatma

B Match the columns. **(1 x 5 = 5)**

Column A	Column B
1. The first tools were made from this	a. *Suwa*
2. Place where fossils are kept	b. Raft
3. Indian name for aniseed	c. *Til*
4. First vehicle used for transport	d. Stone
5. Indian name for sesame	e. Museum

C Find an odd one in each line and write the reason why it is odd. **(2 x 10 = 20)**

1. Fort St George — St Thomas Church — Rock Garden — Snake Park
   Reason: ....
2. Bharatnatyam — Kathak — Chhau — Manipuri
   Reason: ....
3. Letter — Television — Telephone — Email
   Reason: ....
4. *Dosa* — *Thepla* — *Vada* — *Appam*
   Reason: ....
5. Garbha — Bihu — *Pheta* — Rasa
   Reason: ....
6. Rice — Wheat — *Bajra* — Tea
   Reason: ....
7. Coin — Inscription — Monuments — Timeline
   Reason: ....
8. Republic Day — Pongal — Independence Day — Gandhi Jayanti
   Reason: ....
9. Mustard — *Urad* — Sesame — Coconut
   Reason: ....
10. Dhoti — Lungi — *Pagri* — Saree
   Reason: ....

D Answer the following questions. **(3 x 5 = 15)**

1. Did the discovery of fire really change the course of human history?
2. What is the difference between national and religious festivals?
3. Write a note on classical dance and music forms of India.
4. Trace how humans learned the art of agriculture.
5. How did early humans use wheels in different ways?

Notes

Notes

Notes

Notes

Notes

Notes